If every working day makes an eternity in the Ninth Circle of Dante's Inferno seem like a vacation at Club Med . . .

If you'd like to believe that no boss can be so mean, yet you can't deny the existence of that perversely pompous person who's forever on your case and in your face . . .

If you find yourself at the non-mercy of a Mr. or Ms. Boss E. Wrong, who always has to be right, and puts you in the shredder when the worst laid plans hit the fan . . .

Take heart (along with all the other stuff you have to take),

You are not alone. . . .

BOSSES FROM HELL
True Tales from the Trenches

Matthew Sartwell is a former book editor for a major New York publisher. He currently works as a freelance editor and writer—and swears none of the stories in this book comes from his own work experiences. He lives in New York City.

BOSSES
FROM
HELL

TRUE TALES
FROM THE TRENCHES

Matthew Sartwell

A PLUME BOOK

PLUME
Published by the Penguin Group
Penguin Books USA Inc., 375 Hudson Street,
New York, New York 10014, U.S.A.
Penguin Books Ltd, 27 Wrights Lane, London W8 5TZ, England
Penguin Books Australia Ltd, Ringwood, Victoria, Australia
Penguin Books Canada Ltd, 10 Alcorn Avenue,
Toronto, Ontario, Canada M4V 3B2
Penguin Books (N.Z.) Ltd, 182–190 Wairau Road,
Auckland 10, New Zealand

Penguin Books Ltd, Registered Offices:
Harmondsworth, Middlesex, England

First published by Plume, an imprint of Dutton Signet,
a division of Penguin Books USA Inc.

First Printing, April, 1994
10 9 8 7 6 5 4 3 2 1

LIBRARY OF CONGRESS CATALOGING-IN-PUBLICATION DATA
Sartwell, Matthew.
    Bosses from hell : true tales from the trenches / Matthew
Sartwell.
      p. cm.
    ISBN 0-452-27048-0
    1. Supervisors—Humor. 2. Business ethics—Humor. I. Title.
HF5549.12.S26 1994
658.3'02'0207—dc20   93-37204
                                                       CIP

Printed in the United States of America
Set in Garamond
Designed by Eve L. Kirch

ACKNOWLEDGMENTS

I forced many people to relive incidents they would rather have forgotten. I am both grateful and sorry.

I got moral support and encouragement from my parents, Charles and Cheryl Sartwell, as well as my siblings, Ann and Peter. Lynne Mazza, Michael Moore, and Michael Mahana also held my hand when I needed it.

Laurie Bernstein put this idea in my head and made the book possible. Peter Borland kept the ball rolling and generously indulged my tardiness.

There were others as well, people with incredible memories who opened old wounds to help me and to put me in touch with other veterans of the working world. I promised not to use their names, but they know who they are.

CONTENTS

Introduction

• • • • • • • •

The average human being does not consider the word "despot" a compliment, yet some freak genetic mutation must keep the world abundantly supplied with monsters whose voracious appetites can only be sated by feasting on the dignity, self-esteem, and wounded feelings of others.

These are the Bosses from Hell. They're everywhere—in your local libraries, doctor's offices, and coffee shops. They prowl the halls of Corporate America and lurk behind the silver screen. They call you up at two in the morning, they dig through your desk while you're at lunch, and they don't care that they're paying you slave wages. One year, during National Secretaries Week, the newspapers were full of reports about a woman whose boss forced her to take dictation while he sat on the toilet. Let's hope that story didn't give anybody ideas.

You have only two choices when confronted with one of Satan's minions in blue pin stripes. Quit, or tell your story to anyone who will listen. If you disappear while picking up your boss's dry cleaning, at least your friends will know why.

What makes us continue working for these modern-day Simon Legrees? Money, usually, although often it's about half what we deserve. But they can quickly have you under their spell, convincing you that you're just lazy, that *everybody* works an eighty-hour week without complaining. It's only when the drugstore is delivering antacids by the case that you realize things have gone too far.

Bosses from Hell are part of an ancient tradition. Remember Jacob? He worked for Laban for seven years to win the right to marry Rachel, then Laban tricked him into marrying her cross-eyed sister, Leah. So Jacob worked another seven years for Rachel, then six more just to get a decent severance package.

God pity you if you've had to endure twenty years of a jerk. Most of us do break free sooner than that. But even then the jerks may still pursue you, and all the garlic and crosses in Christendom won't put them off your track.

Bosses from Hell are masters of disguise. They can be men or women, older than you or younger. They have an uncanny sense of your weak spots; they know just what to say to bring back all the humiliation you felt when you got that D in algebra. They have no shame, no pity. They take no prisoners.

The tales that follow are true, although the names and some identifying details have been changed to protect the innocent from the guilty. If you're reading along and your conscience pricks you because your name is Lester and you once locked your secretary in the closet for a typo, don't call your lawyer, because it isn't you. But aren't you ashamed of yourself?

1

I'm the Boss, You're Not

No, there isn't a master race, but that information hasn't yet reached your employer. What better reason to do something than simply because you've been told to? Common sense. Compassion. Logic. What are these to someone who's obviously so far superior to little old you? Forget about your grandmother's funeral or your own wedding. Never forget who has the upper hand. Your soul has been sold and you didn't even know it.

● ● ● ● ● ● ● ● ● **I** COME OUT TO CALIFORNIA in '35, and me and my wife, we was stayin' on a ranch where her brother was workin'. And Dorothy, she was pregnant, so I got me a job over at Moss Landing, at one of them sardine canneries. I was working in the fertilizer barn, baggin' up the ground-up leftovers from the cannery.

And this son of a bitch ran the fertilizer barn, he was the meanest bastard you ever did see. There was just me and him in that barn. I come on one day 'bout eight o'clock, and I started baggin' that fertilizer, and long about one o'clock I said, "Hey, I'm hungry. I'm gonna get me some lunch."

And this old bastard said, "No you ain't. You keep baggin' that fertilizer or you don't got no job."

So I kept baggin'. But I was pretty hungry, and that barn *stunk*. And long about five o'clock I said, "Now I'm gonna get me some dinner."

And this old boy said, "No sir. As long as that fertilizer keeps comin', you keep baggin' it."

Well, by this time my hands were all bloody from all those bags, but I kept workin', and this bastard just sat there with his feet up on a can.

By about nine o'clock I couldn't see too good. That old SOB, he decides to go home, and he leaves me there workin'. "As

long as that fertilizer keeps comin', you keep baggin' it," he said.
So I just twisted this here handle on the pipe, and pretty soon
it wasn't comin' no more.

I was still pretty dizzy so I sat down. And these fellows come
runnin' over from the main shed real quick, 'cause there was
fish guts spillin' out of the pipes back there. "What the hell's
goin' on here?" the foreman shouts.

I told 'em about how this boy worked me for thirteen hours
without nothin' to eat and no place to sit down, and I showed
'em my hands, and I said, "You owe me thirteen hours' wages.
I ain't never comin' back here again."

And that foreman, he said, "Wait, wait, wait." And he took
me over to his office, and he fried me up some eggs and bacon
on a little hot plate he had over there. And the next day, *I* was
runnin' the fertilizer barn. I don't know what happened to that
other fella.

—*Charlie, 77, California*

● ● ● ● ● ● ● ● A BIG PART OF THE PROB-
lem was that this was a work-
study job, and it wasn't really clear what I was supposed to do.
I met the guy who hired me at a recycling drop-off, and we
started talking when I was there, and it turned out that he was
the director of this center in the architecture department that was
collecting all this research on solar energy. He told me he
needed somebody to catalog all the research and be sort of a
general clerical person.

For the first term it was great. I shelved books, I answered
the phone, and that was about it. There really wasn't that much
that needed to be done, so I got to study a lot while I was there.
Hey, this was a work-study job, wasn't it?

I was the only person working there who wasn't an architecture student. I was interested in the research, though, because

I'm really committed to the environment, but I didn't get all excited about the mechanics of passive heating or anything. And I could tell that the other architecture students who worked there really felt like I was an outsider, some kind of dilettante. That didn't matter first term, though.

Then the guy who hired me graduated, and he was replaced by this guy named Lance. Lance started giving me all this junk work to do, like I had to fold, label, stamp, and sort for bulk mail two thousand copies of a newsletter. I must have gotten about fifty paper cuts, and it took me a week to finish it because Lance kept coming up with new labels every time I had everything sorted, and I had to go back and re-sort all the bundles that were ready to go.

That's kind of small peanuts, I guess, but Lance was always talking to me in this condescending tone, like I didn't know anything just because I wasn't God's gift to architecture. And whenever I didn't quite understand some esoteric point about cooling systems, he'd decide that meant I must have screwed up the cataloging. I must have pulled everything off the shelves and recataloged it three times.

So, you get the point, he was trying to get me to quit so he could replace me with an architecture student. But the money was good, and I decided I wasn't going to give in, just to spite him.

Then one day, at the end of the term, it was time to send out another newsletter. I had folded almost all two thousand of them and I was tired of it, so I decided to take a break and I started to read the newsletter. Most of it was pretty technical and I just skimmed it. But then on page five there was this box with big black lines around it, and inside was a notice. It said:

"If you're a regular user of the Center's library, we apologize if you've had some difficulty finding materials this year. Our cataloger is a little slow, and she isn't quite up to the task. But don't worry, better minds than hers are now supervising the work, and we hope to replace her soon with a bona fide architecture student with a better grasp of the job."

As if he thought I'd never see it! I thought about pulling everything off the shelves right then and there, and putting it back willy-nilly so they could never find anything again. But I decided to be more subtle. I typed up another note, and I had two thousand copies run off at Kinko's, and I inserted one inside each newsletter. I was there until about two in the morning doing it, but the newsletters went out without Lance ever suspecting. This is what my notice said:

"If you've noticed an awful smell around the Center this past term, we have to apologize for our director. His personal hygiene leaves much to be desired, and the stench can sometimes be overpowering. But don't worry. His mommy has agreed to come live with him and make sure he bathes every day and brushes his teeth after breakfast, lunch, and dinner. In the meantime, a grant from the Ford Foundation will supply nose plugs to anyone who must brave the Center until Lance's mommy gets here."

It took about a week before somebody showed Lance a copy. Sure, I was fired. But hey, it was worth it.

—*Michiko, 25, Florida*

• • • • • • • • W HEN I WAS TWELVE YEARS old, me and my friend Marian would steal money from our parents, cut summer school and go down to Coney Island and ride the Cyclone all day. And this old guy who ran the ride noticed that we were around all the time, and one day he told us, "Stand here and take tickets." And then he disappeared for a couple of hours and came back about dinner time.

So we had jobs as ticket takers on the Cyclone, and we thought that was really cool and really responsible and that we were hot stuff. At the end of the day he would give us each five dollars, and we were happy.

I don't know, maybe the guy wasn't paying off somebody, but this inspector from the city came around and busted us for being underage workers. This was really strange, because all kinds of stuff goes on at places like that that isn't really legal, but that's how they do business. And this inspector turned us in for cutting school and our parents found out and we were in trouble, big time.

But the worst thing was that this guy never let us ride again, even though we bought tickets, and I always thought that was a pretty pissy way to treat a couple of kids who'd worked for you all summer, when all they wanted to do was ride a roller coaster.

—*Don, 38, New Jersey*

● ● ● ● ● ● ● ● M Y ONLY CONTACT WITH Ferris was by letter. I'd agreed to write a science fiction thriller for him, based on some characters he'd created. That was the way he worked—he sold an idea to a publisher and then found somebody to write the book.

I spent three months putting the novel together. I gave it lots of action and exotic locales, with gross-out aliens and technology that made the *Enterprise* look like a Tin Lizzie. And of course some sex. All of Ferris's books had to have sex in them.

I finished up just in time for Thanksgiving and sent it off. The day after Christmas I got a letter back from him, and I forgot all about "ho, ho, ho."

What kind of pervert was I? he wanted to know. Didn't I know how to satisfy a woman? Maybe I'd never had a woman, maybe I didn't even like them. Maybe I preferred garden hoses and things that crawled out of swamps.

Where had I learned to write? From the instructions that came with electronic equipment made in Taiwan? Had I heard of an adjective, did I know what that key on my word processor with a little dot on it was for? Maybe I'd asked my kid sister to write the manuscript in between nap time and din-din. Or had

I just set an epileptic monkey down in front of my keyboard?

I had never been so insulted in all my life. I wrote right back to him and told him that if my writing was so awful he could just pay me the kill fee we'd agreed on and forget the whole thing. I got a check in a week.

I decided to put it all behind me, and I concentrated on my journalism. I sold a few magazine travel articles, and I did a feature interview with a local high school girl who got a part in *Buffy the Vampire Slayer.*

Then one day I was browsing the shelves of my favorite bookstore, and I saw the latest book in Ferris's series. I picked it up and read the back cover. It seemed awfully familiar. I read a few pages, ran to the cash register, paid for the thing, and drove home.

I sat down with my manuscript and started reading. This was my story! Sure, some of the names had been changed and it didn't have my more gripping style, but this was my book! I wrote another letter to Ferris that afternoon and then I called a lawyer.

All I got back was a photocopy of a page out of my contract. Which said that if I accepted the kill fee, then Ferris owned the manuscript and could do whatever he wanted to it. So he'd watered down the story, cut the best parts, added this sappy little love interest, and published it!

The lawyer said there was nothing I could do. Ferris was within his rights. Maybe, but if I ever meet him, I'll show him just what kind of lowlife I really am.

—*Jaimie, 24, Nevada*

● ● ● ● ● ● ● ● **W**HEN I FIRST CAME TO this country, I did not speak English well. I could read it and write it because I had been taught in school, but I did not have much chance to speak English in our little town in Lebanon, and so my speech was not good.

I was hired by a very mean man to work as his maid. He did not pay me very much, and he made me work very hard to do things that did not need to be done. Once he made me move his refrigerator all by myself and clean all the dust from the back. It was very greasy and I could not make my hands clean for several days.

But I would not have cared about the work if he had not done other things. Often he told me I was lucky to work for him because no one would hire an Arab because we were always blowing up airplanes and killing Americans. I was not a terrorist!

He also thought that because I did not speak well I did not understand him when he spoke, so he yelled everything at me, as if I was a deaf person. When he wanted me to wash the windows, he would stand in front of one and make big wiping motions with his hands.

But the worst thing he did was try to teach me English. He thought it would be very funny if I cursed at people. He told me that when I was introduced to someone that I should say, "Fuck you." When someone did something for me, I was supposed to say, "Drop dead, sucker."

I did not do this, because I knew what those words meant, but that made him think that I was even more stupid. I worked for him for only eight months and then I quit when my husband also immigrated to America. We own our own cleaning service now, and I do not think about him much, but perhaps, if I ever meet him again, I will enjoy saying to him, "Fuck you," so that he knows I learned my lessons very well.

—Shareen, 37, Connecticut

● ● ● ● ● ● ● ● ● I WAS WORKING AT A SMALL-
time chain of burger barns,
and small-time pretty much summed up my boss, Claude. I'd
been a shift supervisor for three years when he was transferred
in as manager from another store about fifty miles away. I don't
know why he was flipping burgers, since he drove a flashy car
and acted like he'd been born with a Harvard degree. I was just
paying my rent, but I believe in doing a good job.

I was the one to open up on Sunday; I would come in about
an hour early, fire up the grills and fryers, chop lettuce and
tomatoes, get the cash registers set up. I came in one morning
like usual, except the back door was unlocked, and when I stuck
my head in, I saw that the prep room was a wreck.

Well, I wasn't risking my life for $3.85 an hour. I called the
police. And I called Claude, but he wasn't home, so I called the
district manager. The cops and the district manager came and
found—nothing. The money was still in the safe, nothing was
missing. Somebody had just thrown a trash can full of garbage
up in the air and let it all come down.

Funny thing, it turned out that Claude had been the one to
close up the night before. And when he showed up about five
minutes before opening time, he had a hangover that was so
thick you could cut it with a knife. He wasn't real happy about
the cops, and he sure wasn't excited to see his boss.

Somehow, he explained it all away to them. To me, he didn't
say anything. All week it would be, "Charlie, tell Betty to scrub
the fryer" or "Linda, tell Betty she can take her lunch break at
two."

He wouldn't say hello, he wouldn't even look me in the eye,
like it was my fault he was an asshole. So I got all the junk jobs,
scrubbing everything, taking the last break. I was dreading
Thursday, when it would just be the two of us after nine o'clock.
I got the silent treatment all the way until closing time, and then
he started following me around, inspecting my work.

"You missed a spot on the shake machine."

"Your register's off by $1.32."

I just kept doing my work, trying to ignore him. I could tell that he really wanted me to react, so even though I felt like dunking his head in the fryer, I didn't. Then I made a really stupid mistake. Instead of putting the extra lettuce back in the cooler from the waist-high doors behind the grill, I walked around to the back and in the big door.

The door swung shut behind me, and as I put the lettuce on the shelf, I heard a scraping sound. I turned around and I had this sick feeling in my stomach. He'd locked the door! I was trapped! Then the light went out.

And he was laughing, at least until I heard him go out the back door.

I wasn't trapped actually. I climbed out the front, through the door I should have used in the first place. Then I reached back inside, took out a whole gallon of mayonnaise, and emptied it on Claude's desk.

—*Betty, 36, South Carolina*

• • • • • • • • O LD MR. WHITE, HE WAS A sour old man. Something deep down inside him was plain old mean, and he didn't care if everybody knew it.

I worked on his farm for three years, and come rain or come shine, he wouldn't bend his back to help a man out or see his way to tell you you'd done a good job. In fact, he liked to rub your nose in it when even the smallest things went wrong, and if he had to work to do it, well that was fine with him.

One time I was supposed to go out to a barn way off in the north pasture. Most times I drove the truck out, but we'd had rain for about a week straight, and the ground it was all soft and muddy, so you couldn't take the truck out because it would get stuck, and then you'd have to wait for the mud to dry out before you could get the truck running again.

So I walked out there through mud that came up to my boot tops sometimes. It must have took me near half an hour in the rain. And as soon as I got there I realized I'd forgotten to bring a new salt lick. Mr. White didn't let us keep any extra in that barn because he was tight with his money, and he only bought a new one when the old one was about the size of a nail.

But I went ahead and threw down some fresh hay from the loft, and then I started to shovel out the manure since I was there already. I was mostly through when I saw Mr. White walkin' in my direction from the house, and he was fighting that mud just as bad as I had. It was a lot more work for an old man like him to make that walk than it had been for me.

Well, he finally made it and he came walkin' up to me and he said, "You forgot the salt. Better come and get it."

Then he turned around and started walking back to the house.

Now I ask you, what kind of man would walk all that way to tell a hand that he forgot something and not bring that salt along? But that was Mr. White.

—*Elmer, 45, Montana*

● ● ● ● ● ● ● ● ● I DON'T KNOW WHEN SALLY May rolled down out of the hills, but I'd have been a lot happier if she'd stayed back in Dog Patch and left me alone.

She was the bookkeeper/office manager at the nonprofit fund-raising agency where I worked, and she thought it was hilarious to call herself The Controller, like it was a really clever joke. But it wasn't funny. She hadn't had any experience being in a position of authority before, and she got all her management advice from her husband, who was a marine captain.

Every morning my co-worker, Dolores, and I would have to stand side by side in Sally May's office and listen to her tell us what we had to do for the day. I'd just stand there, looking down into her yammering mouth at her incredibly bad teeth. Sally May had the palest skin and this bright red hair, which she frosted and tortured into enormous curls. They were so big we called them "bomb curls."

Sally May figured that her usefulness in the office depended on saving every penny she could. At one point, one of our workers in the field had a mental breakdown. He started telling people that he'd been engaged to one of the women who died when the space shuttle blew up. He even had a set of blueprints that he said were for the condo they had been planning to build together. It wasn't really dangerous, but it was sad. The first thing that Sally May did when we found out what was happening was call our insurance company and have him taken off the plan. She said hospitalizing him for a mental condition would ruin our premiums.

Sally May hated the fact that Dolores and I were so close. One day she took Dolores aside after I went out on an errand and said, "You know, Mack kind of reminds me of my mongoloid brother, Johnny."

We had a good laugh about that one, especially when we got onto hillbillies and incest jokes.

After that little bit of skilled subterfuge didn't work, Sally May decided she would just fire Dolores. We could tell something was up because she started giving Dolores the silent treatment. Then Dolores's manicurist told her that he'd done Sally May's nails the day before, and she'd been asking all kinds of questions about Dolores.

But the clincher came when Sally May called me in and told me that with such a small staff, it would be really smart if we learned each other's jobs. "What if Dolores gets sick, or wants to take a long vacation? Find out where she keeps things, who she orders supplies from, when things have to be done."

Right. What could be more transparent? Dolores just laughed and said if they wanted to pay her unemployment she'd be a lot happier than having to look at Sally May every day, which is also what she told Sally May when she got the ax.

As for me, I took a week off to go to a wedding in Montreal, and the last day of my vacation I sent them my resignation letter and my key by overnight mail. I bet Sally May had a lot more to say than "aw, shucks."

—*Mack, 32, Texas*

• • • • • • • • **M**OST OF MY JOB IS TRAVeling around to stores in the chain and observing how they're run and making reports back to the main office about how things could be better. My boss used to be this guy named Ed, who was supposed to then help the stores implement the changes.

The chain is spread across five states, so sometimes I was a long way from home, and sometimes I was right in my own backyard. One of the real dogs in the chain was right under our noses, and Ed sent me down there.

I didn't want to go because the assistant manager there was my boyfriend, Greg. I already knew from Greg what the biggest problem was—his boss, Scott. Scott played favorites with the staff, and he was lax about store security. The staff wasn't encouraged to be friendly to customers; in fact, they were downright rude from what I could tell.

But Scott was Greg's buddy, and Greg put a lot of pressure on me not to come down hard on him. I was in a real bind, because if I wrote a vague report, somebody else would be sent down to check things out, and I'd be in real trouble for not noticing these things. After all, it was what they paid me for.

So I wrote Ed, my boss, a very detailed report, and even though I didn't say any of it was Scott's fault, it was pretty obvious. To make my boyfriend happy, I wrote "confidential" all over the report, and I explained the situation to Ed and asked him to do what he could to keep my name out of it. It seemed pretty obvious to me that Scott was going to get canned.

Two days later Greg calls me at home and tells me I'm a backstabbing bitch and that he's breaking up with me. It turned out that Ed had decided that my report was too soft on Scott, so he'd rewritten it, blaming everything on Scott, and sent it to the VP for operations with my name on it. And the VP's secretary happened to be Scott's sister, so she'd told him that I was the one who'd blown the whistle and gotten him fired.

I never could get Greg or Scott to believe me. But I know that Scott's sister is still whispering nasty things about me to her new boss, who happens to be Ed.

—*Janice, 31, Oregon*

● ● ● ● ● ● ● ● F LASH TEMPS WAS A SMALL office just three of us, including Candace. She was all sweetness and light with all the personnel agencies and even the temps. She saved the vinegar for us.

Candace never told you if you'd done anything wrong. She left you a note. You'd come back after lunch and a little note on your chair would say, "I wonder if you could possibly consider showing up on time tomorrow."

Or, "It seems you spent an awfully long time this morning on a phone call that had nothing to do with work. Is this the best use of your time?"

Because the real rush was always in the morning, Candace usually didn't come back after lunch, so if you wanted to say something about her note, you'd have to wait until the next morning, and then she'd say, "I really don't have time to talk about it now, dear. Have you found someone for the Wexlers yet?"

One day she left me a note that read, "Please dress more appropriately for the office." It was out in plain sight where Beth, the other woman, could see it.

I was really pissed. Maybe I didn't dress out of *Vogue* like she did, but I was always neat and professional. I threw the note in a trash can and spent the afternoon fuming.

The next day, after lunch, I found the old note on my chair again. She'd fished it out of the trash and underlined it in red ink. Beth looked the other way when I sat down, and I knew she knew.

I came in early the next day to confront Candace. "What's wrong with the way I dress?" I asked, my arms folded across my chest.

"Well, it's so . . ." She rolled her eyes. ". . . frumpy."

Frumpy!

"I can't afford to shop at Magnin's on my salary," I told her. "And why did you leave this note where Beth could see it?"

"Beth has no business looking at your desk," she sniffed, and she picked up a pen and started to write Beth a note.

"Wait a minute. I want an apology. You're too afraid to tell us these things in private, even if they don't make any sense, but you're perfectly happy to embarrass us in front of each other."

She gave me this haughty look and said, "How I run this business is my business. Don't you have work to do?"

I sat at my desk all morning, snapping at people on the phone. And when I came back from lunch, this time the note said, "You can go home now. You're fired."

—*Joyce, 43, California*

• • • • • • • • • **O**NE: THIS IS A TOTALLY nonsmoking office for everyone else, but Josh owns it, so he gets to smoke. As I sit there, dying for a cigarette, he blows smoke in my face and says, "What's wrong, Janet? You look sick."

Two: There is a time clock, which is totally ridiculous because everyone is on salary. If I am three minutes late from lunch because the line at the bank was so long it took my whole lunch hour to cash my check, I have to stay three minutes at the end of the day.

Three: One week's paid vacation no matter how long you've worked there. No personal days either. If I have to see the doctor, that counts as a vacation day, which must be requested a month in advance. I have not left town since 1989, when I went to Urbana, Illinois, for my sister's wedding. I have two nephews I have never seen and a new stepmother. I think her name is Joyce, or is it Margery? I could check but there's number four.

Four: No personal phone calls. If I get one, Josh will either listen in and start making rude comments or he will come out to my desk and disconnect that call. My husband got hit on the head at his shop and Josh cut the doctor off in midsentence.

Is that enough? Or do you want to hear about the Christmas party at Denny's?

—Janet, 37, Iowa

• • • • • • • • M Y SUPERVISOR, GLORIA, meant well, I'm sure she did, but the problem was she thought she was everybody's mother.

A real camaraderie grows up around nurses who work together for very long. You can't face the kind of stuff you see as a nurse without having some good support, and other nurses are your best bet. They know exactly what you're going through because they've been there, from the old man who pinches you to the woman whose family abandons her in the hospital to the patient who dies in your arms.

We had a great team on my shift. We pulled together, we backed each other up, we even covered for each other when busy-work papers didn't get filled out.

But Gloria decided that I needed a man in my life. Honestly, I didn't want to be dating. I'd been divorced for a year, and I was still unsure about men and what they wanted. It seemed better just to let things be.

Ever heard of a juggernaut? That was Gloria when it came to my meeting a man. She was relentless and unstoppable. At first she would make pointed comments about the handsome guy who was visiting his sister in room 1107. Then she started sending me in to check on patients when they had male guests. But that didn't work because I wouldn't do anything about it when I got in there.

Once, a friend of mine from nursing school showed up to see me because he had an interview at the hospital, and Gloria was fluttering around like a mother hen until she heard him mention his wife, the doctor.

Thus began my saga of blind dates, courtesy of Gloria. I gave in only because there was no other way to have peace. There was this guy from Gloria's church who was so eager to get me into bed that I wondered if he'd ever read the Ten Commandments. Another one smoked a whole pack of cigarettes over dinner. Then there was her nephew, who confessed that he'd been bullied into this as much as I had been and maybe it was time to tell his aunt that he was gay. We actually had a good time, and I think I would have liked him for a friend, but Gloria would have taken it as encouragement.

Then one day this guy moved in across the hall from me, and he was funny, he liked the Kinks, and he was a writer. Pretty soon I was dating him, and now we're engaged.

The only problem: Gloria thinks he's a bum.

—Paula, 32, West Virginia

• • • • • • • • **B**OOK PUBLISHING IS ONE
of those businesses in which
there are a thousand tiny little steps up the ladder. I was offi-
cially an associate editor, and I had been for a year. My review
came around and Meg called me into her office.

"You've taken on a lot of responsibility in the last year, Amy.
In fact, I'd say that you've been doing the work of a full editor
for about the last six months. You're working independently,
you're establishing good agent contacts, and you're bringing in
some exciting projects.

"I'd like to promote you to editor, and as soon as the money
is available I will. You deserve it."

I was elated, although of course what I really wanted was a
promotion right there. But at least I had a commitment.

"However," Meg continued, "I'm not going to recommend
any kind of salary increase at this time. I think you need to work
harder. Just because you're doing the work of a position higher
than the one you occupy doesn't mean you deserve a raise for
the job you're doing. Here, sign your review form."

—*Amy, 32, New York*

• • • • • • • • **Y**OU KNOW WHO SHE IS. I
mean if I even told you what
I did for this woman, it would be so obvious who she was, so
I can't really say why I worked for her, but I did.

She wasn't just mean to me; she was, like, equal-opportunity
mean. There was another lady who worked for this woman, and
this lady's mother died and she took a few days off, and the
woman I worked for would call her up at the funeral parlor

when she was sitting with the body and greeting people who came to pay respects. And this woman would yell at her about all kinds of things that weren't getting done, all while this poor woman's mother isn't even in the ground yet.

And there was this guy who did some creative stuff for us, I can't say exactly what 'cause that would give it away, but he was really smart and later on he kind of became famous by himself. Well, he was gay, and she would make fun of him, not just behind his back, but to his face! She'd wave her hands around with her wrist all limp, and she'd make all these sly comments about him liking boys. He finally just quit and, like I said, he did really well without her.

Oh, she used to throw these enormous fits, and she'd swear like a sailor and she'd throw things. Once she hit somebody with an ashtray and she never apologized; she just yelled, "Get the hell out of my way."

And she was cheap! She was so cheap. She had all this money and she was cheap. If she had some food delivered to the office, she wouldn't let us tip the delivery guys, but we did it anyway out of our own pockets, because otherwise they wouldn't come when we wanted something for ourselves.

She wouldn't pay people she owed money to either. Once there was this guy who had done some work for her, and she hadn't paid him in, like, six months, and he kept bothering her about the bill. Then she saw in the paper that he was doing work for somebody else, and she called that person and told them that this guy had stolen something when he was in her office, and he got fired.

There wasn't anything really big that ever happened to me because I tried to stay out of her way. But it was just amazing how mean she was, like she worked at it and she lay awake at night trying to think of more ways to be meaner tomorrow than she'd been yesterday. I guess that's a talent not many people have.

—Lee, 26, whereabouts unknown

2

It's All
Your Fault

Idiot! Moron! Who told you to do that? Surely it couldn't have been the rocket scientist you work for. Why, a boss is infallible. When it comes to conviction, the Pope doesn't hold a candle to your boss. If something goes wrong, there's only one person to blame, the same person who caused last week's disaster, and the one before that, and the one before that. Honestly, can't you do anything right?

The Saga of Henry, Part I

I T'S A FAMILY-OWNED DEAL-ership, and the problem is that every member of the family is my boss. Cross one of them and you cross them all.

Let's start with Louise, she's the mother. She doesn't really work there, she just owns the property. This is a typical day with Louise: You get to the lot at eight o'clock and you get a message that you're supposed to go over to her house and pick her up. She wants to go into Manhattan to go shopping.

So you pick out the biggest car on the lot and drive to Louise's, and when you get there she comes out and she complains that you're late and the least her two lousy sons could do for their poor mother was to send somebody over in a decent car instead of this heap of junk, which looks like something a black person drives. Which in this case it is, because I am a black person and my fate is to drive Louise.

So we get on the expressway, and Louise is in the back seat. "Slow down! Hurry up! Take this exit! I hate this expressway, take the parkway!" she yells. In between she tells you what ungrateful schmucks she raised since she has to beg them for a little help every time she goes shopping.

When you get to Manhattan, Louise makes you lock all the doors because the criminals might yank them open and steal her fur coat or rape her. You cannot, in fact, drive in anything but the center lanes, because this reduces the possibility that Louise will be assaulted. If you drive down a street with only two lanes, Louise tells you to create your own center lane, which makes you very popular in midtown.

Once you get to the store where Louise wants to shop, you have to be two people, since Louise wants you to wait in the car, which is double-parked, and come with her for protection from the muggers who roam the aisles at Bloomingdales. You are better off if Louise decides you should guard the car, because if Louise wants you to follow her inside you still have to double-park the car and then you get to listen to her moan about the cheap stuff they sell these days and what extortion it is that people should have to pay these prices.

At lunchtime you are lucky if you get to take the bags back to the car. In fact, you are lucky if the car is still there, because often it is towed and then you not only have Louise to deal with, you get to call her sons at the dealership. If the car is there, you must go with Louise to the cheapest diner she can find and sit with her while she tells them to burn her hamburger because otherwise it is disgusting. You are only allowed to eat a salad because Louise does not want to ride with you back to Long Island if you have eaten something which will give you gas.

When Louise has finished sending her hamburger back for the third time so that the cook can make sure there are no juices left in it, and she has eaten maybe three bites of it and told you that no one makes a decent pickle anymore, you take Louise to visit her friend Irene. You must drive to Irene's apartment on the Lower East Side and honk the horn until Irene comes out. You may not ring Irene's buzzer, because while you are out of the car someone might attack.

When Irene comes out you feel sorry for her because she must endure this every week. You drive up Park Avenue to Fifty-ninth Street and over to Central Park. While you make the loop of Central Park, Louise will scream at you not to drive so fast and be sure not to get any horse manure on the tires. Louise will also tell Irene about how successful her sons are and how sad it is that Irene's daughter is only a hygienist. If Louise is feeling particularly compassionate, she will tell Irene she is lucky not to be a widow, and thank God her Sam spared her that when he ran off with that hussy from Ozone Park.

After you have taken Irene home, it is Louise's job to tell you that Irene's life is even worse than you can imagine because her daughter is a lesbian and she voted for Jesse Jackson.

You must not return to Long Island by way of the tunnel because Louise hates being trapped in there and she thinks it is highway robbery to pay a toll. Especially if it is rush hour, you must drive no faster than forty-five miles an hour, because the roads are full of crazy people and no one knows when they will cut you off and cause an accident.

When you get Louise home you must carry her bags into the house and then go to the store for some milk. You may not buy it at the convenience store a mile away because they charge too much, but you do anyway because Louise never pays you for the milk.

Now it is at least four o'clock and you return the car to the dealership. You have not sold any cars, you have made no contacts, and you have earned no commission.

That is a day with Louise.

—Henry, 43, New York

• • • • • • • • • I WAS IN A BACKLOADER that turned over and dumped me. Broke both my legs and it wasn't my fault, because that son of a bitch Miller had me working next to a basement that didn't have no foundation yet, and the wall just gave way and in I fell.

And I'm lyin' there with this backloader on top a' me, and he comes slidin' down what's left of the wall. And what's the first thing the bastard says to me?

"Damn it, Reilly, what the hell did you do to my backloader?"

—Reilly, 47, New Hampshire

● ● ● ● ● ● ● ● N AN SLAMMED DOWN THE phone in Dallas, and even though I was in Florence, Italy, I could hear the way she must have been screaming at anybody who was handy. It had been an ugly phone call, and she didn't want to hear what I had to say.

I was supposed to be arranging a deal whereby Nan's chain of boutiques—the one I was a buyer for—would import a line of Italian leather goods, mostly purses and shoes. The negotiations weren't going well. With the dollar getting weaker every day, the Italians kept raising their prices, and it looked like we weren't going to get a deal.

Nan had wanted me to slip them a little something under the table. "All Italians take bribes," she said. "It's a way of life there." But I had refused. That wasn't the way I did business. I could still hear her yelling at me when I went to sleep.

The meeting with the Italians went really badly at lunch the next day, and I could feel it all slipping away. What was really awful, though, was when my corporate American Express card was declined. I figured it had to be a computer glitch, but I didn't want to look like a bigger fool in front of the Italians, so I didn't make a fuss. I paid for lunch on my VISA, but I'd done a lot of shopping for myself that trip. I calculated my remaining credit limit and figured I had about a hundred bucks left.

When I got back to the hotel, I called American Express to straighten things out. The woman I got was quite polite as she explained that my card had been canceled because the corporation had reported it stolen. I tried to explain that it hadn't been stolen, that it had been issued to me and I still had it. She was very apologetic but said someone in the home office would have to call the United States and would get back to me.

I called Nan right away, even though it was only about nine-thirty in Dallas. She wouldn't take the call. She never did for the next three days, and the American Express people said they had been forbidden to let me charge anything else.

Thank God for my parents, who got me an AmEx card in their name, which the people in Florence had for me the next morning. Otherwise I'd probably still be in Italy, scrubbing pots at the Hilton, instead of suing Nan's ass off right here in Dallas.

—Sondra, 41, Texas

● ● ● ● ● ● ● ● AS ROBERT'S ASSISTANT, I was supposed to write a lot of his routine correspondence, memos, thank-you letters, that sort of thing. My first week on the job I wrote a memo about new quality control measures that would be taken at the plant. I put it together from some notes he'd given me and older memos that had just been proposals.

I wasn't really familiar with all the issues. I don't know much about auto assembly. So I gave him a draft and asked for his comments. He said something about how he hoped I wouldn't have to run every little thing past him, but he'd look at it.

The next morning the corrected memo was on my desk with comments scribbled all over it. "No, no, you've got it all wrong," said one. Another read: "You missed the whole point." He'd fussed with the punctuation and changed the spelling of three or four words that were actually correct. I grimaced, but I started retyping.

About ten o'clock the interoffice mail came around. And there was my memo. He'd had it copied—with all his nasty notes—and sent it to everyone in the office!

—Peggy, 52, Indiana

● ● ● ● ● ● ● ● ● ● ● **I** WAS WORKING AT A stock-photo house—the kind of place that has pictures you can use for an ad or something, and all you have to do is pay a fee.

There's a lot of paper work involved, because every time you let somebody use a picture, you have to keep records of what it was used for and then update the national system so that somebody else doesn't use it for the same kind of thing. One time this airline used a picture of a beach in the Caribbean for one of their ads, and it turned out to be the same picture that another airline was using in their magazine. Everybody was pretty upset.

So, my boss is this woman named Tricia. And all Tricia ever did was talk on the phone to her boyfriends—she had a lot of them at the same time—and do the crossword puzzle. She was always buying these magazines of really easy puzzles, and all day long all you'd hear from her was, "What's a four-letter word for island?"

It's really hard to say why all of a sudden a place like that gets extra busy, unless the Olympics happen and then everybody wants pictures of Spain. But it happened a lot, and we'd get swamped because there were only four of us.

When we got swamped, Tricia was supposed to take care of checking out whether a picture had been used before and how. That way, she could still talk on the phone and she didn't have to be nice to our customers. But sure thing, she was real sloppy about it, and finally we sold this romantic picture of two people having a candlelight dinner for an ad agency to use for a fancy hotel.

It took about a month, but right after the ad came out somebody at the hotel found out that the same picture had been sold for this video company to use on the box for a soft-core porno movie. I guess there wasn't anything really romantic in the movie, so they just pretended on the box.

And the shit hit the fan. The ad agency called our main office in New York, and there were all these phone calls because the people in New York wanted to know who was responsible. And that lazy bitch just pointed her finger at me and said, "Her."

Luckily, I got another job in the art department of a magazine, but whenever we need stock photos I tell everybody to stay away from Tricia or their romantic country shots will end up looking like some X-rated movie.

—Ann, 28, Illinois

● ● ● ● ● ● ● ● ● I AM A LIMOUSINE DRIVER, and very often I drive important people. Government ministers, writers, rock stars. Many big people come to Munich, and I drive them.

But she thinks she is important. She is a *diva*, an opera singer. No one else is ever so rude to me.

We are on the *autobahn*, traveling maybe a hundred kilometers an hour, which is not fast for that road. My telephone rings. It is Mr. Sloane. He is the diva's manager. He is calling from New York City.

"Would you please slow down!" he says. "You are making Miss Harpy nervous with your reckless driving!"

—Jurgen, 39, Germany

The Saga of Henry, Part II

• • • • • • • • **M**OST DAYS YOU DO NOT have to drive Louise. Then you must stay at the dealership and work with Louise's sons. Their names are Arthur and Ronald, but this makes no difference because they are exactly the same, except that Ronald has a mustache.

If you approach a customer and they express interest in buying an automobile, you know that somewhere a secret radar is alerting Arthur or Ronald. When the customer decides to take a test drive of the car, one of them will appear and enact scenario A or scenario B.

In scenario A, Arthur or Ronald will be very jovial and will ask the customer how you have been treating them. You will then be told that you have a phone call in the office, which you do not. You will, however, go to the office to answer this phone call anyway, and if you ever see the customer again it will be when they bring their newly purchased automobile in for service.

In scenario B, Arthur or Ronald will sadly explain that the particular car the customer is interested in has just been sold and suggest that a dealership in Freeport might have something similar. You will not see this customer again, and if you do, you are to act busy when they ask for help. Arthur or Ronald's powers of salesmanship have alerted him that these individuals are chronic browsers and not worth your time.

Rarely, Arthur or Ronald will be so busy that neither scenario comes to pass. In this case, you may actually persuade the customer to make an offer.

The offer will be too low. Arthur or Ronald will tell you to respond with an offer one hundred dollars below the sticker. If the customer does not leave at this point, or at each successive point at which you come down one hundred dollars or less, Arthur or Ronald will eventually instruct you that the difference between the price he wants and the price the customer has offered will come out of your commission. You do not encourage trade-ins, because they are losers on the lot.

If you are lucky and the deal is made, you will find that your commission is roughly half what you hoped it would be.

This is a day with Arthur or Ronald.

● ● ● ● ● ● ● ● ● N ICK ACTUALLY HAD THE nerve to call the place the Continental House of Pancakes, as if that fooled anybody. It was a miserable little truck stop really, and it served only three kinds of pancakes and one kind of waffles, so we had a lot of disappointed customers who wandered in off the interstate.

Everything about Nick was cheap and seedy. We'd take a gallon bottle of syrup, pour it into a pot, heat it up, add some food coloring and a gallon of water, and serve it to the customers. They complained all the time.

He was always trying to cut corners. When it was slow he would make a bunch of pancakes ahead of time, throw them in the freezer, and then just heat them up on the grill when it got busy. The only problem was, it took just about as long to heat them up as it did to cook them, and the customers complained about the way they tasted on top of everything else.

I didn't work in the kitchen much actually. Most of the time I waitressed, and working those tables was like walking a mine field, because you never knew when some customer was going to lose it about the stuff he found in his sausage.

Naturally, business stunk most of the time. Nick decided to save his business by having an "all you can eat" special. For $6.95 you could have all the pancakes you could choke down. It was a pretty good deal, since a stack of four cost $4.95, and sure thing, it brought in a lot of business.

But Nick was so cheap he started getting all worried about

how much food he was shoveling out for a measly seven bucks, and he did all kinds of things like start making the pancakes smaller on the reorders and taking a really long time to put them up.

Of course he wasn't the one getting yelled at by a bunch of truckers, and our tips really stunk when some guy decided he'd been ripped off. I got stiffed a couple of times every day, which was a big chunk out of my take-home.

These two really big guys came in together one day. I could tell by what they were saying to each other that they were taking a couple of semis up to Vancouver, and they'd been on the road for about ten hours without stopping. They ordered the special and they kept sending the plates back for more.

I went back to the window with the plates for about the seventh time and Nick said, "Uh-uh, no more. I'm cutting those guys off."

"Nick," I said. "You better not. There's gonna be trouble."

"No more. Go tell 'em."

I went back to the table and I told those guys that they couldn't have any more.

One of 'em stood up. He was only about two times as tall as I was and he looked like he could put his whole hand right around my throat. "Listen, sister, that sign out there says 'all you can eat,' and we ain't done eatin' yet. So bring us some more hot cakes real fast."

I almost ran back to the window and I told Nick what they said.

"Throw 'em out."

I said, "You can't be serious. They'll kill me."

"Tell 'em to pay up and get out, D'Ann."

So I practically crawled back to their table and I said in this tiny little voice, "The owner says would you please pay your tab and move along."

This time both of 'em stand up, and one of 'em knocks his chair over. He decides this is a good idea, so he knocks the table over, too. The other one grabs me by both shoulders and yells, "Tell me who this piss-ass manager is."

I look over at the kitchen and I see that Nick has run out to see who's smashing his fine china. It feels real good to point in his direction and say, "Him."

—*D'Ann, 31, Utah*

● ● ● ● ● ● ● ● Somebody SPILLED LIQUID dog vitamins on the floor, and I stepped in it, and whammo! I fell and hit my head and got a concussion and optical neuritis, which meant I was essentially blind for about six weeks.

So finally I recover enough that I don't get dizzy every time I stand up and I can focus on things more than two feet away from me. And now it's time to go back to work, except that while I've been on disability, my old boss at the pet shop has been fired and there's a new manager.

I go in to work for the first time again on Christmas Eve because they're supposed to be really busy. But instead of putting me to work, the new manager pulls me into her office and proceeds to tear me apart. She tells me she's had all these problems since she started and they're my fault. And she says I've been faking my injury and I've been trying to rip off the company. In fact, even though I've never met this woman before in my life, she tells me I've done all this just to spite her—and that I'm fired.

Merry Christmas.

—*Anne Marie, 26, Montana*

● ● ● ● ● ● ● ● When CLIFF QUIT IT WAS disappointing to all of us. He'd been the manager of the museum's bookstore for almost eight years, and I'd never had a job I enjoyed so much. It was a good place to work, quite easygoing. Cliff had a true interest in offering the customers unusual items that reflected the museum's focus on American arts and crafts, and he encouraged all of us who worked for him to find things that might sell in the store.

Cliff's replacement was a young woman, Sherry. I'm not familiar with her background; I only know that it was evident she had worked in a museum with a much more upscale interest. She began replacing honest-to-goodness craft works with cheap reproductions of high-art items, and we started stocking books about floral arrangements and herb gardens. Gustav Stickley went out the window, replaced by Mario Buatta.

But Sherry's real fear was Cliff's reputation. She refused to use his office and had a much larger stock room remodeled for her own, and we had to crowd the back stock into Cliff's old office.

She was determined to erase Cliff's memory from that store. All the old memos about procedures and policy were thrown out and she wrote new ones, sometimes changing just little things, other times throwing out completely good systems merely to show us that she was the boss. She raised the prices. She doubled the handling charges for mail orders. She even once told us that we should "forget" to give members their discounts unless they reminded us. You can imagine the to-do that caused.

One day during the Christmas season the store was very busy. We ran out of a certain set of earrings behind the counter, and Sherry asked me where to send someone to get more. How she thought she could be the manager without knowing something that simple, I don't know.

Without thinking I replied, "They are on the shelf next to the light switch in Cliff's old office."

Well, she simply blew up. She turned on me in front of a good dozen customers and began to yell. "That isn't Cliff's old office, it's the stockroom, the *stockroom*, damn it! Cliff is gone, can't you get that through your thick head? He's gone, gone, gone, and I'm the manager now, you stupid cow!"

I do not have to take that sort of treatment from anyone, let alone someone who is nearly half my age, but because we did have customers in the shop and I do not like creating scenes, I simply replied, "I beg your pardon," and returned to helping a gentleman at the cash register.

But Sherry was not satisfied with her outburst. "Don't get snotty with me. I've had just about enough of your high-and-mighty ways," she retorted. "Go home, just go home and get out of my sight!"

I certainly did, and I'm pleased to say I have never laid eyes on that woman again. The museum closed the shop within a year and replaced it with a café.

—*Charlotte, 64, Washington, D.C.*

The Saga of Henry, Part III

● ● ● ● ● ● ● ● ● **W**HEN YOU DO NOT HAVE to drive Louise, and Arthur or Ronald has sent you to the office for a phone call you do not have, you will encounter Jennifer. Jennifer is the office manager; she is the daughter of Arthur or Ronald, it does not matter which.

Jennifer is young and beautiful—everyone knows this. It is ultimately unfair that Jennifer must work as an office manager at the dealership when all her friends get to have cool jobs in advertising. Jennifer's friends get to drive Lexuses or BMWs, not cruddy American cars, which are uncool.

Jennifer will tell you about the party her friend Monica had last Saturday—it was a blast. Jennifer must live at home; she does not have a condo, a major injustice. Barry's father bought him a loft in SoHo, which is way-hoppin' and a total blast. Jennifer's father is an old fart. He does not understand what a young woman needs to be happy.

You will tell Jennifer that you must return to the floor because scenario A has been completed. Jennifer does not allow this. She is lonely in the office, and her old man has practically chained her to this desk to answer stupid phone calls. Jennifer will get a phone call, but it will not be from a customer, it will be from Jody. You will try to slip away, but Jennifer will wave you back and you must sit until Jody has finished telling Jennifer about her trip to St. Martin.

Jennifer never gets to go to St. Martin. She is only allowed to go to Miami twice a year. Once she had to go to Fort Myers with Louise, which is a totally dead place. You will agree that going anywhere with Louise is a hard experience. Jennifer will tell you you don't know the half of it, but hey, what's wrong with her grandmother? You had better not be saying anything bad about her grandmother. She owns this place and she could throw us all out on our butts if she wanted to.

The phone will ring again, and Jennifer's face will tell you that it is a customer, because customers always complain. Jennifer will schedule the customer for a service appointment in a week and a half, and do not bother to ask about a loaner in the meantime, because there isn't one. What is this, a charity?

Jennifer will realize that she is out of cigarettes. It is your duty to sneak out of the dealership and purchase Jennifer's cigarettes. You must not let Arthur or Ronald discover you doing this because Jennifer is not supposed to smoke. When you return with the cigarettes, Jennifer is not expected to pay you for them. You must then accompany Jennifer out behind the building where she will smoke three cigarettes in rapid succession. She will not offer you a breath mint when she is through; after all, it is your clothes and not your breath that will give you away to Arthur or Ronald.

But Arthur or Ronald does not need to smell your clothes, because Jennifer's brother or cousin, Andy, who runs the service department, will report her. Arthur or Ronald will come running out and will snatch Jennifer's cigarette out of her mouth and stomp on it. Jennifer will burst into tears because it is her life and she ought to be running it. She will stalk back to the office and treat customers as if it were their fault she is not allowed to smoke and must be a slave in an office.

Arthur or Ronald will yell. You are encouraging Jennifer's bad habits. You should just watch out, buddy, because you are sure as hell not good enough for Arthur or Ronald's daughter, who is destined to marry a man whose last name ends in M.D.,

D.M.D., or Esq. Your wife will be relieved to know that you are forbidden to fool around with a woman half her age.

Now it will be five o'clock. You have not spoken to a customer since Arthur or Ronald took over. You have met no new customers, and you have earned no commission. This is a day with Jennifer.

• • • • • • • • R ALPH HAD THESE GIGANtic hands, like he could crush a watermelon in one. And he always waved them around, especially when he was shouting. Which was often.

He was also a liar. I was his secretary, and it was my job to keep the world at bay. I said he wasn't there, I said he was in a meeting, I said he was on the other line. I told his wife that he was in New Orleans when he was in Miami with another woman. I told the other woman that he was out of town when the wife got suspicious.

And I hated it. I couldn't remember who I'd told what. I knew nobody believed me, that they all thought I was as big a liar as he was. Since I almost was, I felt pretty lousy.

One day his boss called and dutifully I said, "Just a moment, Ms. McPherson, I'll get him for you." She was only five offices away and he was just walking up to my desk. I told him she was on the line.

"Tell her I'm not here."

"I already told her you were in your office." Which wasn't really true, but I had to take a stand somewhere.

"Tell her you made a mistake."

"Ralph, she's not going to believe me."

And his eyes got real big, like bull's-eyes. And his face got all red, and he pointed one of those big, long hairy fingers at me and screamed, "When I tell you to lie, you lie! You work for *me*! I own you!"

And wham! his finger comes down on my desk like a ruler.

"Now, tell McPherson I'm not here."

My hand was shaking as I reached for the phone, but Ms. McPherson wasn't on the line anymore. She couldn't be. She was standing right behind Ralph. And the only thing I heard her say to Ralph was, "I'd like to talk with you a moment, *slave*."

—*Dora, 29, Oregon*

● ● ● ● ● ● ● ● WELL, YOU KNOW THAT mostly I do couture, not off the rack, and when business was better I had plenty of my own clients. I didn't really want to go to work for someone else, but I'd been sick and I needed to start working again.

The woman who hired me was Dawn. She was very funny and we laughed a lot during the interview. She and her partner were doing these upscale women's clothes. She said they wanted to glorify their design and I would just be perfect for that. I wanted to wait another week because I was still taking medication and it made me all fuzzy, but she said they were just desperate. So I said I'd start tomorrow but I might only be able to do a few hours for the first couple of days. Dawn said that was fine.

I got there and Dawn wasn't in. Instead, I had to start working with her partner, Camille, who was a real battle-ax. I introduced myself and she said, "So you're Bob, huh?"

My name is Bill. Dawn had told me that I'd have an office, but Camille takes me to this table surrounded by about fifty other people, including this kid who's playing hip-hop on his radio, and tells me this is where I'll work. Then she comes over with a couple of sketches and says, "Here, clean these up."

Now excuse me, but Dawn had told me that I was supposed

to be designing on my own. And I told this to Camille, and she says, "Listen, Bob, just do it."

"Bill," I tell her.

"Whatever," she says, and she walks away.

So I take a look at the first sketch, and it's for a full-length coat. It looks like a sausage. It has no waist but very tight cuffs, big shoulders and a tiny collar, and it's drawn in at the hem. My style is very sleek and elegant, and this certainly is not sleek and elegant. Besides, no woman can look good when she's dressed like a sausage.

I try to make it better, but I mean, hey, you can't make a silk purse out of a sausage, which is what it still looks like after two hours. And now it's very hot, and my medication is making me very dizzy.

So at lunch Dawn still hasn't come in. I go over to Camille's office and I tell her that I have to go home now. "What about those sketches?" she barks. I show her the coat and she says, "That stinks."

"Yes, I know," I tell her, and I say that maybe I can do some work at home.

"Well, hurry up," is all she says.

So the next day I come back, and still no Dawn. The coat still looks like a sausage but more like a hot dog now than a baloney. And Camille walks over and hands me three more designs that are even worse than the coat. "I need these by lunch, Bob," she tells me.

So lunchtime comes and the coat still looks awful and there's no way I can save any of the other designs either. Camille comes stalking over, like she can smell blood.

"This isn't going to work," she says in front of everybody else. "You're too fussy. Get out of here."

So I left. At least she got my name right on the measly check.

—Bill, 55, New York

● ● ● ● ● ● ● ● ● ● **I**T WAS MY FAULT, I GUESS, though I didn't write the thing. Still, I was the publicity assistant the agency had review the program, and the offending lines had been there staring me in the face. Still, I do think it was something of an overreaction.

Hildegard Bumpkus was one of our major opera clients—a big woman with a big voice and a big following. She was easily one of the top five sopranos in the world. She was giving a dual recital in Philadelphia with another soprano, also a big talent. I'll call her Brunhilde Burrito. There was more than a little rivalry between these women. Divas are like Siamese fighting fish— you can't have two of them in the same tank for very long before warfare breaks out.

It was about an hour before the concert was to begin. Ms. Bumpkus had just arrived and swept into her dressing room. "Hello, orchestra!" she had trilled with a little wave of her hand as she passed two violinists in the hall. "Hello, publicity!" she said as she saw me.

Her manager was with her, a fat, nervous little man who kept rubbing his hands together as if he were thinking of all the money she made for him. Leo. I hated him almost as much as I feared her.

She'd been in there about ten seconds when she let out a screech. Sopranos do that well. The dressing room door flew open and she stood there with a program clenched in her hand. She was trembling. She stalked forward and thrust it under my nose.

"This is an outrage. I simply cannot perform under these circumstances. Since when is Burrito a *Madame* when I am only a *Miss*!"

I wanted to melt into the wall. Of course I knew right away that's how the program referred to them. It hadn't really caught my attention, but I guess I remember thinking that since Burrito was about ten years older than Bumpkus, it seemed right.

Leo had followed her out. There was sweat on his face, and

I imagined it was pure smarm, just oozing out of his skin. "Audrey, how could you have let this happen? This is a serious insult to one of our most valuable clients. You idiot."

"I . . . I . . . I'm sorry," I gasped, lying through my teeth. "It's just that Ms. Bumpkus seems so much younger. I thought *Madame* would make her seem as old as Ms. Burrito."

Bumpkus's eyes showed a brief moment of triumph then went narrow again, as if she were a cobra facing a mongoose. Leo just hissed. I looked to my left and about ten feet away, there was Burrito.

—*Audrey, 27, Pennsylvania*

● ● ● ● ● ● ● ●   S O THE PHONE RINGS, AND it's *Mrs.* Winchell and she wants to know if Mr. Winchell is in. And I say, "No, he's not." And she says, "Where is he?" And I say that he's gone to lunch with the lady manager of that factory he owns in Mexico.

And then she starts talkin' real fast and pumpin' me for information about him and her, and what time she got there and what time they left, and how long's she stayin' and where is she stayin', and what does she look like. And I'm talkin' as fast as I can, and then all of a sudden she hangs up.

See, what I don't know is that Mr. Winchell has been screwin' this lady from Mexico, and Mrs. Winchell found out about two years ago. And he made her this promise that he'd stop foolin' around and he'd sell the factory 'cause their marriage meant more to him than money. Only he hasn't, and he's been sneakin' this woman into the country 'cause he can't go to Mexico anymore, see?

This is what I find out from Mr. Winchell when I get to work the next morning, and he chases me out of there with a stapler, as if this was all my fault. I was just being nice to his wife.

Only it isn't enough that he scares me out of my job. He starts callin' me at home and leavin' me these messages about how he better not ever see me again or he'll mess up my face. And he tells me he's got friends who get mad whenever he gets mad, and maybe they'll pay me a visit. I know what that means, 'cause I grew up in the Bronx.

Well, maybe I was just a typist, but I knew a few things about takin' care of myself. And a long time before I left that place I brought home a box of these light bulbs he was makin' in Mexico. On the side of the box it says "General Electric Quality Bulbs." And on the top of the bulbs, instead of just GE it said GEQ. Now he would tell you that "General Electric Quality Bulbs" only meant that they were just as good as any GE light bulb, which they weren't.

But I called him up and I said, "Listen, mister, I got an uncle who works for General Electric, and if you don't leave me alone and if anything ever happens to me, he's gonna get those light bulbs and that great big company is gonna squash you like a bug."

Which was a lie, because my uncle owns a Jiffy Lube in Ronkonkoma. But hey, it worked.

—*Tracey, 22, New Jersey*

The Saga of Henry, Part IV

● ● ● ● ● ● ● ● **D**ESPITE THE BEST EFFORTS of Louise, Arthur or Ronald, and Jennifer, sometimes you will sell a car.

Something will go wrong with this car. The muffler will fall off, or the brake lights will not light on one side. The customer will brave Jennifer and get a service appointment sometime after the next full moon. The customer will bring in the car in, and the customer will meet Andy, who is the brother or cousin of Jennifer and the son or nephew of Arthur or Ronald.

Andy hates people who whine. Customers by definition whine. Your customer will seek you out when Andy tells them to keep their pants on, for chrissake. You will attempt to speak with Andy about the customer's complaint. Andy will tell you to fuck off, because his grandmother owns this place and she could have you out on your ass in a second.

The customer's car will be returned after Andy or one of his buddies has had a chance to take it out to the expressway and see what the baby will do with the pedal to the floor. Sometimes a motorist will file a complaint about the driver in the coupe with license plate AAA 555. This is not, however, a problem because no one can prove that Andy was driving that car and the cops will just nail the customer, who is a whiner.

The customer's car will not truly be fixed on the first attempt and it will have to be brought back. At this point, Andy will discover that the heating system is about to blow, and the customer will not see the car again until the heating system is no longer necessary because everyone is using air conditioning. The customer will not be happy. The customer will, in fact, begin using the word "lemon," and there is a law about that in this state.

Andy will tell the customer to drop dead. The customer will complain to the Department of Consumer Affairs and the dealership will be forced to compensate the customer. This is your fault, because this is precisely the kind of situation scenario B is meant to prevent. You should not have sold that customer a car in the first place, no matter that you had made no commissions in two weeks. You will be docked that commission out of your next two commissions.

You may have sold this customer a car once, but you will not sell that customer a car again because you are obviously in league with management. Perhaps the customer will complain about you at the next dealership and when you interview there for a new job, they will tell you that you have a bad reputation and customers will not trust you.

This is a week with Andy. You have sold one car, but you will never sell a car ever again. You are lucky your wife is a therapist.

● ● ● ● ● ● ● ● ● ● ●**I**T WAS SEVEN-THIRTY IN the morning and I was in the ship's galley, stuffing a big cloth bag with old vegetables, broken plates, and a twelve-pound roast that was supposed to look like a head. Thanks to my boss.

I'd been a purser on the S.S. *Adelaide* for seven years. When the previous chief purser retired, I figured I was in line for his job, but instead the cruise line brought in Barry. He found out pretty quickly that I thought I deserved his job and he made my life hell. I ended up with the midnight shifts on the cheap decks. I was always on duty during port calls, so I didn't leave the ship for weeks at a time, and I couldn't do anything right. Every time I turned around, there was Barry, complaining about my uniform, apologizing to the passengers because I hadn't jumped when they snapped.

The worst duty was burial detail. With a few thousand passengers, a lot of them old folks whose doctors had advised them to travel for their health, it wasn't unusual for someone to die while we were at sea. Most of the time we emptied a deep freeze and stowed the corpse there until we got back to our home port. But sometimes the spouses would decide a burial at sea would be romantic, and we became funeral directors.

Burial was a simple event, always held early in the morning so we wouldn't upset the ship's festive mood. The captain or the chaplain would officiate, and after a short service the body, wrapped in a white shroud, would be tilted off a special platform and into the briny blue.

I'd had to oversee three burials in two months, and at the last one the platform had stuck. We'd had to use some real muscle to send our departed passenger on his way. The widow had been more than a little upset, and Barry blamed me.

When Mr. Peabody died of a massive coronary in the saltwater pool, Barry assigned me burial detail again. "Don't fuck it up this time," he sneered.

By seven o'clock I had everything together for the eight

o'clock service, and a few other crew members and I were marking a respectful vigil when Barry walked up. He straightened the flag over the body, rearranged the flowers, and flicked some imaginary dirt off my shoulders. "I hope this goes off well," he sniffed. "We have to do everything possible for our passengers in times like these. We have to show them the utmost respect. Does that fucking platform work?"

"Yes, sir," I replied. "We oiled the mechanism and checked it thoroughly."

"That's what you told me last time." And he turned, released the safety catch, and lifted the platform. He probably only meant to test it, but the thing moved like it didn't weigh a pound.

Whoosh! Splash! There went Mr. Peabody, straight for Davy Jones's locker, forty-five minutes early, without benefit of clergy or the comfort of his grieving widow. We stood there for a minute or two, just staring, and then Barry was screaming.

So there I was, trying to create an all-new Mr. Peabody, one who looked roughly like an overweight eighty-two-year-old man and who was heavy enough not to come bobbing to the surface, since the bereaved loved to look over the railing and watch the point of impact recede. A pot roast would have spoiled the effect.

I finally managed to fill up the shroud and lug it back up to the deck about ten minutes before the service. This time everything went off without a hitch. Mrs. Peabody told the captain it had been a lovely service, and the captain complimented Barry on his good job. When we got back to port, I quit and became an Amway salesman.

—*Ray, 50, Texas*

3

You're in the Way

Feeling pretty confident about your work? Think you've finally gotten the hang of things in Con fusion Central? Watch out, you've just become dangerous to someone whose existence depends on the smoke screen you've just penetrated. Bosses from Hell know how to deal with upstarts like you, though. If they strike while you're still enjoying the view, they won't have to worry about you again for a long time. Maybe never.

●   ●   ●   ●   ●   ●   ●   ●   S UMMER STOCK IS EITHER A complete delight or sheer torture. I was in my third season working with a small regional theater in the Midwest when I was selected to portray Blanche in *A Streetcar Named Desire*. At the time the director was a woman with whom I'd worked many times, and I was sure we would do a wonderful job.

But a week into rehearsals this woman's husband was killed in a car accident, and she withdrew, understandably. Her replacement was the theater's other director, a man named John. I had never worked with him—in fact I avoided it—because John was a man of foolish ambitions and very poor taste. That same season he was directing a production of *The Importance of Being Earnest* set in Harlem, an odd mix if ever there was one.

John was having an affair with a woman named Donna, who had a small part in *Streetcar* and was also my understudy. He seemed determined to force me out of the role and move Donna into it. He screamed at me during rehearsals, made me stay after all the others had gone, and changed my blocking almost daily. But after all, I've spent many years in the theater, and I have been bullied by directors before.

When all this didn't work, John began to grow more extreme. He told me I needed to gain fifteen pounds so that Blanche would be zaftig. This would make her seem more vulnerable, he said, and make Stanley's attraction to her more "mysterious." I politely refused, pointing out that I would next be playing Elvira in *Blithe Spirit*, and a zaftig, flirtatious ghost would not work.

He relented on this point but continued to press others that were just as ridiculous. Instead of a genteel Southern accent, he wanted cornpone. He proposed that Blanche limp, again to make her seem more vulnerable, and the next day wanted to add a stutter.

He placed me in precarious positions on the set and instructed me to engage in wild histrionics that would have sent me tumbling to the stage. Maybe an injury to the lead was the best way for the understudy to succeed to the role.

The worst was the costumes. Everyone else was to be attired very typically in working-class clothes. But for Blanche he had the wardrobe mistress assemble a wild collection of leopard prints, slit skirts, and sheer blouses, which he told me I should wear without a bra!

I refused this flat out, and he burst into a tirade about my refusal to work with him. "Who the hell do you think you are, Jessica Tandy? Every step of the way you've fought me on this production. Now wear those clothes or you're out of this production!"

So I was fitted with these ridiculous clothes, and they made me so self-conscious I was a wreck in rehearsal that day. In at least three places I found that John's blocking left the audience with a clear view right up my flimsy skirt. A member of the lighting crew told me that whenever I stood in the doorway, the skirt became completely see-through and he could tell I was wearing low-rise panties.

All my protests did no good, and I made it through the last few rehearsals with my teeth gritted. On opening night, the first two scenes went well, but then I made an entrance through the famous doorway, brightly lit by an arc from stage right. And the audience gasped, then burst out laughing as I stood there in my gauzy blouse and sheer skirt, practically as naked as the day I was born.

The headline in the local paper's review the next day was "BLANCHE DU BOIS AS YOU'VE NEVER SEEN HER BEFORE."

—*Inez, 40, Maryland*

● ● ● ● ● ● ● ● ● ● I WAS SEDUCED BY THE glamour of it all. I was twenty-three, in the big city for the first time, and this was maybe *the* most famous advertising agency in the world. I didn't even know if I wanted to work in advertising, but all my friends did, so why not.

Our biggest account was a cosmetics manufacturer, and I was their day-to-day liaison. I got along great with their people and everybody I worked with. The only problem was Sid. I think maybe he was a little jealous of my good relations with the client. After all, he was the actual account executive, but I was the one they called with questions and instructions. It probably didn't help that I was gay, and Sid did everything he could think of to let people know he was straight, right down to ogling the secretaries where everybody could see him.

Anyway, the time came when we presented a campaign—six magazine ads—and the client hated it. They'd already turned down the last concept, and at the end of the Friday meeting their marketing VP, Judy, said to me. "Well, Larry, let's see what you can come up with by Monday."

She said it to me, not to Sid. I could practically see the steam coming out of his ears as soon as we were alone. "All right, Mister Popularity," he hissed, "let's see what you can come up with by Monday!"

"Me?" I squeaked. I wasn't the creative type.

"Six ads. Monday morning, nine o'clock. Or *else!*" And he stomped off.

I drove my friends crazy that weekend trying to come up with the mother of all lipstick campaigns. A couple of the other people in the office offered me a little encouragement but no real help. They were like rats, deserting a sinking ship. "Luscious, lovely, lips from . . ." I wrote. "He's putty in your hands with . . ." They were stinkers. I got about three hours of sleep, drank a barrel of coffee, and showed up at the office on Monday with the sort of campaigns that would only sell product if you were Darin Stevens and your wife was a witch.

"This is pathetic," Sid told me. "They'll never go for these."

"I told you . . ."

"What makes you think you belong in advertising? Just because you like to use this stuff doesn't mean you can sell it!"

I just clammed up. I couldn't believe he'd said that. Why he was willing to sacrifice the account just to get back at me, I don't know. But he sure had something to prove.

The stuff was cleaned up, and we took a cab over to Judy's office. Sid was obviously determined to sink me. He told Judy how these ideas were my brainchild, how I'd been so enthusiastic about them that the agency had put aside another idea to work these up. He did an excellent job selling her the stuff before he handed it over. I could see why he was an important account exec.

I could also see from Judy's face that no one else in America was going to get a look at my ad copy. She was polite, but she almost looked hurt. It took about two minutes for her to announce she was putting the company's business up for review, and we were ushered into the hall.

We were not alone in the elevator when Sid started to lay into me. The other two people tried to shrink into the corner, and I was praying the cables would snap and it would all end in a thundering crash. There was spit flying from his lips, and his ears were so red that the little white hairs looked like down.

I can't remember exactly what he said except that I was fired. There weren't all the laws about wrongful dismissal in those days, so he didn't need to have written proof of anything. I cleared out my desk that afternoon, and I went home.

The silver lining was that my phone rang two days later. It was Judy. She'd heard what had happened . . . and she offered me a job.

—*Nate, 52, Oklahoma*

● ● ● ● ● ● ● ● ● ● **I**N THE SHOE BUSINESS THE products keep changing all the time because everybody's trying to stay ahead of the competition with some fancy new feature. Most of these changes don't make much difference at all to the customers, but they mean big new prices.

The Sweat Sock was a chain of athletic-shoe stores, and their specialty was selling customers the most expensive shoe on the market. It didn't matter that somebody could get just as good a shoe for half the money; you were supposed to sell them the new model with the Mexican jumping beans in the insole so they could jump higher and pay more money.

Cliff was the living embodiment of this philosophy. I had been working at the store before he was transferred in, and I had built up a good clientele of serious athletes who would come to me for advice. They were really good repeat business, and since we were mostly paid on commission, I valued the fact that they came back to me whenever they wanted new shoes.

But Cliff watched me like a hawk, and he was always complaining about how I didn't sell somebody a shoe that cost a hundred dollars instead of one that cost sixty. "What kind of profit do you think the company makes on a lousy sixty-dollar shoe?" he'd say. And I'd try to tell him how much profit the company made on people who came back every couple of weeks, but he wouldn't listen.

So he started horning in on my sales, and I was helpless. I'd go in back to get a pair for somebody to try on, and I'd come back and Cliff would be talking to them and telling them they really needed the Torpedo with a helium tongue and little sails in the ankle. I'm exaggerating, but you get the point.

So my customers started to go away, because no matter how much they liked me, they couldn't stand him. And if one person at Sweat Sock was so obviously trying to fool them into buying the wrong shoe, why should they trust anybody else there?

Pretty soon I was hardly making any commissions at all and

my sales volume was practically negative, and that gave Cliff a good excuse to cut my hours, which meant my sales dropped more, which meant more hours cut, and so on. One week I came in and he simply hadn't scheduled me at all.

I did confront him, but he told me I just didn't have the Sweat Sock spirit and he could make a lot more money with other people on the floor. He offered me a job working in the stock room, but when I figured out I'd make less money doing that than I had been making in the last couple of weeks, I decided to cut my losses and leave.

I got my revenge on the company later, but not on Cliff, because he'd quit, too. There was this nosy reporter for a local TV station, and she'd heard this rumor about unscrupulous selling practices at Sweat Sock. Was I interested in talking? You bet.

—*Lourdes, 28, New Mexico*

● ● ● ● ● ● ● ● R EMEMBER THAT OLD LINE about not engaging in a battle of wits with an unarmed opponent? That's what I thought I was getting into with Audrey. Was I ever wrong!

She was my boss, the only executive assistant in the firm, and the rest of us were secretaries. She'd been around a long time, and she had just the right look for a very respectable law firm —real traditional, the friendly grandmother type. But she could turn into a mountain lion if she thought one of the partners was threatened by a nosy client. Or if she was in danger of losing power to some uppity kid.

Our battlefield was the new computer system. This was about fifteen years ago when a lot of people weren't used to computers, and I was the only secretary in the office who had serious experience with them.

All the partners were for it except Mr. Woodrow, who was the founder. But even he could see that computers were needed, so they decided to go ahead. I would be working with Mr. Scranton on setting up a system.

All of a sudden Audrey's back was against the wall, because I would be making decisions about new procedures. Procedures! They were Audrey's stranglehold on that place. She knew where everything was, what had happened with it, and what was supposed to happen with anything new. I don't know why she couldn't see that she was still valuable to the firm even if we could survive when she took a day off, but that was the way of it.

First she started telling everybody these horror stories about systems that crashed, killing every piece of data. Why, it had happened to her friend Gwen at the phone company. What a disaster that had been.

After I got everybody calmed down again with talk of hard copies and backups, we picked out a system and it was installed. I was supposed to teach everybody how to use the word processor first; things like spreadsheets and billing would come next.

Oh, that Audrey, she was a tricky one. She actually got the hang of the basics quickly, and then she was giving all kinds of advice to the others, stuff that would screw up their correspondence or save it into the wrong directory so it would take hours to find it. I noticed that none of her work ever got lost or fouled up—until something had to be done right away for one of the partners. Then everything would go wrong, and she'd pat her Selectric and say, "Fortunately, we haven't completely given up on things that are reliable."

So I was looking pretty foolish, especially because things were happening to the system that I couldn't understand or fix. Now, a new system usually has a few bugs, but we were looking at a real disaster, and Mr. Scranton made it clear he thought I had let him down and made him look bad. If he was worried about looking bad, you can imagine how I felt.

About three months after we got the system, there was a big hullabaloo about some pro bono work the firm had done, and one of the trustees of the nonprofit foundation we'd been doing it for made some very serious charges in the newspaper that we'd caused them all kinds of damage because we'd mishandled it. A judge got involved pretty quickly because this involved a bequest from an estate that was still in probate. Of course, everything had been done correctly, right down to the letter, and all we had to do was produce the paperwork and the firm would be cleared.

Sure thing, the system went haywire as soon as we started to retrieve documents. We did have paper copies of everything we'd put into the system, but they had to be found and collated the old-fashioned way, and by the end of the day, Audrey was practically preening. I heard Mr. Scranton say that maybe we ought to just scrap the whole system. I was miserable because I could feel every pair of eyes in the firm boring into my back as I sat at my terminal and tried to recover everything.

It didn't work, and I was starting to admit to myself that I was in way over my head and maybe Audrey was right. But I don't give up that easily. That night at home I called my friend Roy, who taught computers at the community college, and asked him to meet me at lunch the next day. Maybe he could figure out what went wrong.

We met at a restaurant a few blocks from the office, a place where most of the secretaries went regularly. We were just catching up with each other when I saw him wave at someone.

I turned, and there was Audrey standing in the doorway. She went kind of pale, made a feeble wave back, and then ducked out the door again.

"That's my boss. Do you know her?" I asked Roy.

"Sure," he said. "She's one of my best programming students. Say, why don't you get her to help you with these problems? She's got a really good eye for bugs in a program."

Didn't I know it.

—*Mary Ellen, 53, Kentucky*

● ● ● ● ● ● ● ● **L**UCY WAS VERY THREAT-
ened by the fact that, as her
assistant, I was getting attention from other executives and establishing good relations with our clients. This was at a midsize
marketing research company, small enough that the people at
the top knew who you were but big enough that they didn't
encounter you all that often.

Lucy's boss liked me and told me I was a very perceptive
researcher. He asked me to give a presentation on some of our
focus-group findings to a couple of higher-ups. Lucy kept telling
me horror stories about how people got ripped apart in these
meetings, but whenever I'd ask her for advice, she'd smile and
say, "I'm sure you'll do fine."

So I was sort of panicked about this presentation, but I prepared myself really well. Beforehand I got my hair trimmed and
had my nails done, and I came to work dressed very profes-
sionally. I usually did these things anyway, but I wanted to be
sure I made a good impression.

So the meeting started, and I got up to make my presentation.
I was about thirty seconds into it when Lucy reached over and
took my hand and said, "Claire, you got a manicure!"

Her tone of voice was like I had just given birth, she was so
in awe. I was completely embarrassed and felt my face go beet
red.

I kept going and finished the presentation. Just as I was sitting
down, Lucy leaned over to me. In a voice that everyone could
hear, but as if she were talking to me in complete privacy, she
announced, "Very good. See, I told you it wouldn't be so bad."

I really couldn't believe she was doing this, using these supposed compliments to damage me, but nobody else seemed to
notice. Everybody started talking about the report, and every
time I tried to respond, Lucy would interrupt and say something
like, "What Bob means is that he wonders whether you've taken
into account people's willingness to speak honestly about these
issues."

So once again she acted like she was being helpful but was actually humiliating me.

So I never got a word in edgewise, and everybody started talking to Lucy and asking her questions instead of asking me. I was completely out of the discussion.

Finally it ended, and as I was walking to the door, determined to get out of that room, I heard Lucy say, "Claire, that suit does wonders for your figure."

And they all laughed.

—*Claire, 27, Ohio*

● ● ● ● ● ● ● ● T WO GLORIOUS WEEKS IN Italy and I love the world. People are friendly, the earth is beautiful, and I don't even care that I have to go back to work.

At least not until I get to my cubicle and there's another woman sitting at my desk. I say, "Excuse me, I'm Linda Day. This is my desk," and she says, "Not anymore, honey. This is my job now."

And I go to my boss, and he says, "We couldn't afford not to have someone doing your job while you were away, so we hired Agnes." Which is pretty assertive for my boss, who could be Mr. Milquetoast's timid brother. And I've seen Agnes, and judging by her bra size, I wonder about the quality of her trademark research.

But worse: "I'm sure you'll find something else. Personnel will fill you in on the severance package."

Now I don't know what to think. I'm shaking. I'm in shock. I stagger down to my friend Cal's cubicle and he takes one look at me and says, "Welcome back. How's it feel to be replaced by the boss's mistress?"

I tell him I've been fired and he laughs. "Honey, you aren't fired, not unless you want to own this lousy firm. You can sue their ass halfway to Toledo."

Which is right, and it takes me about ten seconds in the personnel office talking about my lawyer before Agnes is packing her purse and snapping her gum at me.

And you'd think that would end it, except that I'm still working for a man whose brain is south of his navel. He just seems real embarrassed at first, but then all of a sudden, I'm calling around town to find out who carries a particular kind of marble countertop, and do they have Poggenpohl cabinets, and can they dye drapes to match carpet. Because since Agnes doesn't have a job, she gets to have an apartment.

And my punishment for taking her job away from her is doing all the grunt work for the decorator and the remodelers. And where can you find antique butterfly cases, and isn't there someone in all of Chicago who has a wing chair covered in raw silk, and, and, and . . .

I should have stayed in Italy.

—Linda, 25, Illinois

4

The Ridiculous Obsession

Of course it's important that every envelope be opened from left to right. The entire world order depends on it. Can't you see that kind of system has made your place of employment the great place it is today? And why shouldn't you listen to fishing stories from 1951? You never know when that kind of information could come in handy. If Albert Einstein never combed his hair, imagine what a real genius should be able to get away with.

● ● ● ● ● ● ● ● ● **W**HEN MY BOSS HAD HIRED
me as an actuary for Enor-
mous Life Insurance, the last thing he said was, "Mr. Sherwood
prefers that the men wear hats."

At first I thought it was a joke. There were even articles in the
paper about how President Kennedy's not wearing a hat at his
inauguration a few years before had been the death knell for
the men's-hat business.

So I didn't do anything about it, just showed up my first day
respectably dressed in an overcoat and conservative blue suit.
But in the elevator on the way up to personnel, I noticed all the
men wore hats. And the closet where everyone hung their coats
was full of hats. It made me a little nervous, but Mr. Sherwood
was the division VP. He wasn't even on our floor. There were
about thirty workers in a big room, each of us crunching numbers. Who would notice me?

I made it through week one, but on the way to lunch that
Friday, Bill, who sat at the next desk, said real offhand, "What'd
you do, forget your hat?"

I still wasn't convinced, but later that afternoon Mr. Sherwood
came round, and my boss introduced us. He was not exactly
dapper. His suit was too short in the sleeves, and he looked like
he slept in it. I figured maybe the hat business was an inside
joke, like everybody was making a little fun of him. He shook

my hand and launched into a little welcoming speech that sounded pretty rehearsed.

Then, just about the time I figured he was done he said, "You'll find that we have standards here at Enormous. Our employees are gentlemen, and we expect them to dress as such. A hat, sir, is the mark of a gentleman. There is no more distinguished item in a man's wardrobe, no better statement you can make about yourself and your company, than to wear a hat. See to it that you do."

Joke's over. This guy is serious. I meant to go out and buy one over the weekend, but I had a date and my mom's car needed tuning, so I didn't get around to it. Monday morning I headed in to work a little early; I figured I'd slip out a little early for lunch and pick one up. Wrong.

Just as I was walking up to the building, a taxi stopped about ten feet ahead of me and out got Mr. Sherwood. He took one look at me and said, "Your hat, sir! Where is your hat?"

I stammered something about having forgotten it, and from the look on his face I might as well have said I forgot to put on my pants. "In the future, sir, you will see to it that you do not come to work without a hat!" he snorted, and stalked into the building.

Damage done, but like I said, all I needed was a chance to get to Altman's at lunch. Wrong again. About ten o'clock I noticed a couple of women from the typing pool going desk to desk, handing out a memo. As soon as I got mine, I took a look. It was from Mr. Sherwood, re: hats.

And it wasn't just an abstract rhapsody. A new employee (I was the only one) had disregarded Enormous's careful traditions. He had behaved thoughtlessly, disgracefully even. A hat was a badge of distinction. Wear it or else.

I could feel dozens of pairs of eyes boring into my back. I heard a couple of snickers, and Bill was leaning over from the next desk to say something when he stopped and straightened up, fast. I followed his eyes, and there was Mr. Sherwood, advancing from the elevators. In his hand was a big, red dunce cap made from construction paper.

He stopped in front of my desk, extended the dunce cap, and announced, "Your hat, sir."

I just stared at him, but he reached out, stuffed it onto my head, and walked away.

I bought two hats at lunch.

—*Walter, 49, Connecticut*

● ● ● ● ● ● ● ● ● ● I HADN'T GROWN UP IN A religious house, so I didn't pay a lot of attention to strict Jewish law; I didn't even know much about it. When I started working for Lenny, I learned a lot because he was very observant, kept kosher, and observed every holiday. He even wore a yarmulke that had the name of our company stitched on the top.

We went out to Pittsburgh to sit in on some focus groups, and our plane was scheduled to bring us back to New York on Friday at one. Lenny had wanted an earlier flight—it was winter and sundown came early. He was always home before the Sabbath began.

Well, the plane was late coming in, then we finally got on, then taxied out to the runway—and waited. It was after two-thirty before the pilot came on and told us that La Guardia Airport was very backed up because of heavy rain, and we'd just have to wait a little longer.

The flight attendants had served us soft drinks, and Lenny was twisting his napkin round and round, fidgeting. "Sarah," he told me, "I have to be home before sundown."

I didn't know exactly what the consequences would be if the weather kept conspiring against us, so I asked.

"I will absolutely lose my mind if I'm on the plane when the Sabbath begins," he said. "I will stand up in the aisles and start to yell and scream. I will throw things. I will make everyone here absolutely miserable."

"So why don't you get off and go home tomorrow night?" I asked.

He looked at me like I'd discovered the cure for cancer. We talked to the flight attendant, and they let him off the plane and agreed to give him a flight the next day. I went home.

—*Sarah, 31, New York*

● ● ● ● ● ● ● ● ● ● I ANSWERED A PERSONAL AD in the back of the paper. Not my normal style, but there has to be a first time for everything, okay? The guy in my ad was sandy-haired, about ten years older than me, "very good looking," and he liked to ski. Sounded good.

I wrote him a really nice letter. I told him all about myself, that I liked to ski, I found older guys attractive, and I was a concierge at a hotel downtown. I signed my full name and included a picture.

I got a great letter back, very smart and kind of funny. But he only signed his name Ted and he didn't send a picture. So I kind of blew it off. I mean, if a guy's so scared of sending you his picture, it makes you wonder, okay?

A week went by and I got another letter from him, wondering if maybe the last one he sent got lost. This one talked about how rich he was and all the places he liked to go, like Aspen and Sugarloaf and San Moritz.

So I was a little more interested and I wrote him back, but I said I thought it would be nice if he sent along a picture and maybe told me his name, since I'd done the same for him. I didn't get a reply, so I figured it was a zero.

Okay, so all this is happening and I'm still working at the hotel. I'm a concierge, but there are usually two or three of us on duty, and my boss is this guy named Carl. He's kind of prissy, like he's watched too many movies about fancy hotels and thinks he's something special because he's been getting people tickets to Blazers games for twenty years. He's always hitting on the women, but nobody will have anything to do with him because he's such a priss. Plus, he's balding and he smokes and he's just kind of gross.

I'd told another woman that I worked with about Ted, but she's such a gossip, and pretty soon everybody was ragging on me about it. Like I'm desperate, which I'm not. Carl didn't say anything, though, because he thinks "that kind of talk doesn't have any place at work."

Pretty soon I got another letter from Ted, and this one had a picture in it, which looked like it was a few years old. He said his last name was Sparks, and he was sorry he'd been such a dweeb about writing, and maybe we could have dinner. He named a date a few weeks ahead and said he'd pick me up at my house.

I called directory assistance, and they said they did have a number for a Ted Sparks, but it was unpublished. So I figured the guy was for real, but he obviously had a few problems about getting close to people since he was still using the box at the newspaper. But what the hell, it was just dinner, right? So I wrote back and said, sure, why not?

I didn't get a new dress or anything, but I did get my hair cut, and by the time the date came I was pretty excited. The doorbell rang right on time, and I opened it—

—and it was *Carl*!

—*Faith, 32, Oregon*

• • • • • • • • • • **I**N MY INTERVIEW EVELYN'S first question had been, "When did the Civil War end?" And what she really wanted was a *day*, not a year. Maybe if I was supposed to be a history teacher I could have understood that, but for a job as an assistant licensing manager?

I got the job, even if I only managed to come up with 1864,

which I gather was the closest anyone got. Evelyn told me one guy answered 1812, so I could see how the question weeded people out.

On a business level, Evelyn was terrific, I can't deny that. We were working for a movie studio, and they held the rights to all kinds of characters and names and things like that, and she was extremely astute. We made good money for the studio.

But every day I had to listen to her rant about the ignorance of young people today, and she was always popping these little spot quizzes on me. "When was the Hundred Years' War?" "Is a whale a fish or a mammal?" "Who wrote *Paradise Lost*?" At least all those nights watching *Jeopardy!* weren't a total waste.

Her biggest hang-up was math. She would go on and on about people who couldn't figure percentages or do long division in their heads. This had more to do with the job, because a lot of licensing has to do with being paid a percentage of the take from a product that uses your stuff. We sometimes made out pretty well because the people we were dealing with didn't realize how much they were going to have to shell out until the time came to write the check.

Evelyn had strong opinions on everything, though. One day I was sitting at my desk eating my lunch and reading a copy of *Vanity Fair* and Evelyn walked by.

"I can't believe you're wasting your time with that rag."

"This? I like it—good dirt."

"Hah! It's nothing but the *National Enquirer* on more expensive paper. They think they're so sophisticated and glamorous, and all they do is print pictures of Madonna with no shirt on."

"I don't think they take themselves so serious—"

"Give it to me!"

"What?"

"Give me that magazine. I don't even want to see it in my department."

I handed it over and she stomped out to our secretary's desk and threw it away. Later, at the end of the day, I tried to fish it out of the garbage, and I heard Evelyn yell from her office, "Leave it alone!"

So I had to buy another copy on the way home. Pretty soon I couldn't read *Los Angeles Magazine* (a bunch of greedy social climbers) or *The New Yorker* (pretentious literary hogwash by a bunch of intellectuals who were playing a big trick on the whole country by pretending that boring ruminations on geological faults or vegetable markets in Hong Kong were significant).

My friends in other departments thought this was pretty hilarious, although I felt like I was working in the Hayes office. On my birthday they threw me a party at lunch, with a cake and champagne in my office. Evelyn came, because it was pretty hard for her not to notice the festivities going on next door. She had a couple of glasses of champagne, and pretty soon she was tipsy. We had to take the cake knife away from her because she was gesturing with it wildly and almost took out somebody's liver.

I got some presents, the usual office gag jokes. One of them was a stack of magazines: *Vanity Fair, The New Yorker, Los Angeles Magazine,* and a couple of *Playboys.* You should have seen Evelyn's face!

Almost as soon as I'd unwrapped them, she lunged across the desk and grabbed about half the stack. "Oh, no!" she slurred, "not in my offith."

I tried to get them back, and everybody was laughing. At first I thought she was making a joke, too, but she wouldn't give them up. Then she noticed that everybody was laughing at her and she yelled, "Out! Ever'body out of thith offith right now. Go back to your deths. Party's over!"

And so all my friends had to shuffle out and leave me alone with Evelyn. She stood there, kind of swaying from side to side, and gave me another big lecture. At the end I said, "You know, you're really just a control freak. These people were just giving me a harmless birthday party, and you've ruined it. Why don't you just leave me alone for the rest of the day so you don't ruin my whole birthday."

She looked real guilty and she kind of slunk out of my office and shut the door real gently. I called my friends at their desks, and we had some nervous laughs about it, and I stayed in there with the door closed for a couple of hours.

After a while I started to feel a little guilty. I mean, Evelyn was drunk, and I knew she didn't know what she was doing. I figured by this point she had probably sobered up and I ought to go make peace before I got a phone call and had to recite the Gettysburg Address.

So I opened my door and walked over to Evelyn's. Then I just stood there, because she was bent over her desk, looking at pictures of Rosanne and Tom Arnold mud wrestling in gold bathing suits.

—Cesar, 26, California

● ● ● ● ● ● ● ● ● **I**'VE CLEANED HOUSE FOR A lot of famous people. Some of them were upright folk, and some of them were just oddballs. But the worst of them was this TV fella. When you saw him on TV he was all masculine and rugged-like, but at home he was like an old woman.

Everything had to be just so. If I moved some clothes in the closet when I vacuumed, I had to put 'em back just like I found 'em. If the flowers on the table faced a particular way, I had to set 'em down the exact same way after I was done dustin'. I had to polish the dishes after they come out of the dishwasher so there wouldn't be no spots. And every day I had to rub a little bit of cologne on the telephone so that when His Highness picked it up, it smelled all nice and sweet.

Each week was supposed to be a different cologne. There was a little line of bottles in the hall cabinet, and they had to go in order. It was Aramis one week, then Lagerfeld, then Halston, then Paco Rabanne, then I don't know what. That man had more cologne than that Marcos woman had shoes.

One day he was all out of somethin'-or-other, whatever was the special of the week. So I went to his bathroom and got the little cotton ball wet with some of the same stuff. I perfumed the telephone like always and went on about my business, but I guess I forgot to put the bottle back. 'Cause the next day he was waitin' for me when I showed up. His lips was real tight and he was all stiff, like somebody stuffed a broomstick down the back of his shirt. And he had that little bottle of cologne in his hand.

"Margaret, what's this?"

I just looked at him for a second, 'cause I wondered if this was a trick. "It's your cologne," I said.

"That's right. And did you take it out of my medicine cabinet yesterday?"

"I did. There wasn't any left in the bottle in the hall."

"Did I tell you to take cologne out of my medicine cabinet?"

"No, sir, you didn't. But you did tell me to rub some on the phone every day, so that's what I did."

He sighed real hard, and I kinda got the idea that he felt like he was talking to a child. "Margaret, this is a serious violation of trust. I cannot have you rummaging through my things looking for whatever you need."

"I wasn't rummaging. I knew what I wanted and I got it. If you don't want me to put that stuff on the telephone every day, suits me just fine. My husband thinks I'm carryin' on with some other man."

I was tryin' a little joke to maybe loosen him up, but it didn't work.

"Is that what you want, Margaret? Do you want to have an affair with me?"

You can see how far off his rocker he was. I just looked at him and said, "Honey, you ain't half the man I need."

So he fired me.

—*Margaret, 65, New Jersey*

● ● ● ● ● ● ● ● T HE FIRST TIME I SAW THE *Saturday Night Live* sketch with the "Pat" character, I thought it had to be written by someone in my office. Someone who knew Terry.

Ambiguous sexuality rolled off Terry like beads of sweat. He—at least we knew that much—was always touching himself, always whining about things in a voice that was like nails on a chalkboard. He hovered over everybody in the office, male and female, staring at us, watching us. His wife was a real bovine, a two-hundred-pounder. She would drop by the office in these ugly sweaters that were unforgettable. Two weeks later, Terry would wear the very same sweater to work.

In addition to being creepy, Terry was vastly unqualified to be the head of marketing research for a division of an agricultural chemical company. He knew nothing about farming, nothing about science, and frankly, nothing about marketing. He solved this problem by doing nothing. Meetings lasted for hours and nothing was ever resolved or implemented, all because Terry didn't want to be bothered to take charge and make decisions.

But it was the creepiness that we had to deal with every day. Everybody had a story to tell, about being trapped in the elevator with him, about seeing a gerbil cage in his trunk. Mine was the day when he called me into his office and shut the door. Terry had this trick of calling everyone in, one by one, to ask what he should do about a "problem" employee. It was his way of spreading gossip.

But my treat was different. He smiled at me and my skin crawled. He slowly opened a desk drawer and took out a book that he'd wrapped in brown paper that looked like a cut-up grocery bag. He opened it up, glanced down, then looked at me and said something.

I couldn't understand him. He repeated himself, then added, "That's French."

"What for?" I asked innocently.

Something that's illegal in 34 states.

Terry had bought a book of French swear words. And for the next hour he proceeded to read me every term in the book. Almost all of them had to do with sex. He rolled the words around in his mouth, as if just saying them in French was as good as committing the act. Sometimes he'd close his eyes after a really juicy translation and shudder a little.

I tried to escape, I really did, but every time I stood up, he'd order me to sit back down. By the time it was all over, I was literally sick to my stomach.

Nobody else admitted to getting that treatment, but they were all just as repulsed as I was. I got my revenge, though, about a week later, when the heifer/wife showed up for lunch. She and Terry would always come back and sit in his office after they ate. Once they'd left, all I had to do was go into Terry's office, take the book out of his drawer and put it on the little table next to the guest chair in Terry's office. It was right next to where the missus would sit.

She found it. And she never let him wear one of her sweaters again.

—*Abe, 31, Idaho*

● ● ● ● ● ● ● ● Mr. PRESCOTT RAN A VERY small but prestigious publicity agency. Mostly we handled classical musicians. For a long time he and his wife had been very social, throwing formal parties and entertaining in their home. Then she died, about a year before I met him, and he was lonely.

Well, the best way he could think of to meet people was to interview them. He could relate to people who needed him; he could get into power. Every few months he'd decide that we needed another person, and he'd put an ad in *The New York Times*. He'd interview all these people and then decide he couldn't afford to hire someone.

One day he decided that I needed an assistant. So we put an ad in the *Times* and he told me to call the recruiting agencies. And I called and said, "Hi, I'm calling from Prescott Associates, and I need to hire a publicity assistant." And they *laughed*.

But they sent people. And I saw a couple I liked. There was one guy named Benny Hwang. He was just out of college, and he'd come to New York from California. He was all right but nothing out of the ordinary. I wanted to hire this woman who'd already done a publicity internship with one of the big management agencies. But Mr. Prescott had seen this guy waiting in the lobby, and he decided Benny Hwang looked like the kind of guy he wanted to hire.

I tried to talk Mr. Prescott into hiring this woman, but he wouldn't make up his mind, and I kept interviewing people and sending the ones I liked to see him. But he didn't like any of them and finally he just called the recruiter and told him we wanted to hire Benny Hwang, and they should send him back for one more interview.

Well, Benny Hwang had been in New York for about three months without finding a job, so he had gone back to California. And the recruiter called him out there and said, "Prescott really liked you. They sound like they want to hire you."

And so now Benny Hwang is calling me and talking about moving back to New York and how he's trying to get a cheap fare because he hasn't got much money left, and he's all excited about working for Prescott.

But Mr. Prescott is starting to sound like he has before. Maybe we can't afford this. Maybe we should all just work a little harder and we won't need to hire another person. I keep trying to put Benny Hwang off, but he's calling me every day and all of a sudden he's got his ticket—nonrefundable—and he's flying in tomorrow.

Of course, ten minutes after I'm off the phone with him, Mr. Prescott walks in and says, "I've decided not to hire somebody else. Call that fellow in California and tell him we won't need him."

So, for Benny Hwang I'm the would-be boss from hell. But he should know what he escaped from.

—*Luann, 28, New York*

• • • • • • • • • • **S**OMEBODY SOMEWHERE had once told Anthony that he knew how to write, which was a big mistake, because he doesn't. He's always editing the memos I send out, insisting on these ridiculous changes. For instance, "Employees whom wish to take the Friday preceeding Memorial Day off must notify this department previous to that point in time."

This might not be so bad, except I work in the personnel department of a newspaper, and a lot of people at newspapers know how to write and they know a mistake when they see one. Besides, everybody hates personnel and they love it when we screw up.

Anthony's speech is even worse. He makes up new malapropisms every day. I started keeping a list. Here are a few:

> Don't look a gift horse in the eye.
> He was running around like a chicken with a head.
> Honey doesn't grow on trees.
> That's bark on the wrong tree.
> You can't make a silk purse out of a cow, dear.
> A hopscotch never boils.

It's like he never really listens to anything people are saying, let alone thinks about what he said actually meant.

Needless to say, there are all kinds of screwups as a result. The worst one came when I got promoted to assistant personnel manager, and that meant I finally got to have business cards. Anthony ordered them, and when they came in they said:

> *Rhonda Pennington*
> *Ass. Personnel Manager*

It took three weeks to get new ones.

—*Rhonda, 27, Michigan*

● ● ● ● ● ● ● ● *C*ASTELL WAS A SMALL LIT-
erary magazine of some re-
pute. Keith and Donna were the publishers, and I was the editor,
working on a volunteer basis because the magazine was mas-
sively in debt and couldn't afford to pay anybody. If things got
better, I would get a salary. I also hoped the prestige and con-
nections would help in my own attempts to sell my novel.

Donna was the day-to-day manager; Keith mostly supplied the
money. They had a rocky, messy relationship that was supposed
to turn into marriage, but it never quite happened. In my opin-
ion, the big obstacle was the fact that they both felt free to sleep
around. Some lusty encounter would lead to weeks of bickering
or worse.

The biggest flare-up came after a local literary conference
sponsored by the university. Donna started flirting with this professor from Ohio, and by the second day of the conference,
everyone knew they had slept together. Keith was furious. He
grabbed me the day after the conference was over and told me
that if Donna kept this up, they were through and he was cutting
off the money for *Castell.*

Of course, this made me angry, because I hadn't spent the
last year and a half working six nights a week just for my health.
Then I heard that the professor was thinking about coming to
our little town on sabbatical the next fall. So I took matters into
my own hands. I called him up and told him just what he was
jeopardizing and that he should stay away.

So Donna hit the roof. Her lower lip was trembling as she
bawled me out, telling me to quit sticking my nose in other
people's business. And when I told her that if her wanton ways
were undermining all my hard work it *was* my business, she
turned on Keith.

There followed an enormous fight in her office. She screamed,
he yelled. Somebody threw something. Then silence.

Then, "Oh, Keith," "Oh, Donna," "Oh, baby," and a lot more

silence. Finally they both came out, their clothes all rumpled, and Donna said, "Leslie, I think it's better if you don't work here anymore."

The ingrates! After all I'd done for them.

—Leslie, 38, North Carolina

● ● ● ● ● ● ● ● L EONARD DID THE FISH and I did the frogs. He was in charge of all the research animals used in the university labs, but he was obsessed with the fish room. I guess that's what twenty years of the same mindless work will do to you.

The fish room was temperature-controlled because some of the species were very rare and fragile. Leonard guarded them like they were gold. He didn't even like it when the professors went in. He'd follow them around, cooing at the fish and talking to them, telling them the big bad men weren't going to hurt them. None of the rest of the maintenance staff could go in without him.

The problem was that the tanks often overflowed and the drain in the floor couldn't handle it. The ceiling of the teaching lab downstairs would start to leak, and some snotty grad student would come up and start cussing at us for ruining his experiment. The first time it happened, I went in and mopped up all the water. When Leonard found out, he went crazy. He tried to hit me with a mop and told me that he'd kill me if I ever went in there again without him.

So the next couple of times I just called Leonard at home and waited for him to show up while these grad students kept calling me names and complaining about union rules. The union didn't have anything to do with it. I just didn't want to have to face Leonard.

Finally it happened again, and I called Leonard, but he wasn't home. I just went back to my other work while the students got all huffy and important. One of them went away and came back with the head of the biology department. He told me if I didn't go in there and stop the leak right away, he'd have me fired. I believed him.

So I got my mop and went to the fish-room door. I could imagine what Leonard was going to say, but I put my hand on the knob, pushed the door open and stepped in.

And wham! this big metal bucket comes down from up above and hits me on the head, spilling putrid fishwater all over me. Leonard had booby-trapped the place!

I should have let the biology guy go in first.

—Joe, 41, Massachusetts

● ● ● ● ● ● ● ● ● **I**'LL JUST SAY THAT SHE WAS a well-known performer. And that her weight was almost as well-known as her other talents. She'd finally gotten it down to a very attractive range.

I was one of those publicity flacks hired to stand around backstage and keep the crowds of adoring fans at bay. Tonight she was feeling gracious and had agreed to sign autographs. I stood there with an armful of publicity photos, all of them brand-new, showing off the now-svelte star.

There was a long line of autograph hounds. Some of them had programs or other paraphernalia they wanted her to sign, so I didn't pay much attention when this meek little man refused the picture I handed him. He got to her about a minute later and stuck out another photo that he'd been clutching.

She went white and let out a screech they must have heard on the street. "Marty! Marty! This is one of my *fat* pictures!"

And she lifted it up over her head and ripped it into tiny little pieces, then threw it at the guy's feet. End of autograph session.

I've still got the fat picture though. I saved the pieces and taped them back together. I framed it and hung it over my toilet.

—Marty, 28, Florida

● ● ● ● ● ● ● ● ● IT'S A FANCY DINNER PARTY for twelve, and we're catering it from the kitchen of a big house out in Germantown. Lots of gold jewelry on the women and plenty of BMWs in the driveway.

Linda's take on this whole thing is that it's her big break. All these people here throw lots of parties, and if we make a splash she's sure of lots more jobs. I don't like working for her since she doesn't really know anything about food, just about how to set a pretty table. She thinks she's Martha Stewart. In fact, I'm pretty sure that the table laid out in the dining room is the same one Martha set on page 73 of one of her books.

Almost everything is going fine, except that Linda's dogging my every step. The chicken breasts are under the broiler, just to brown for a second; the wild rice is just finished and I'm fluffing it with a fork, and my assistant is draining the asparagus. He's just served the seated guests a salad of endive and walnuts.

"What about the chicken?" Linda asks.

"I'll give it another minute," I say.

"It's going to burn," she insists. And she bends down and opens the broiler. "Just in time," she announces triumphantly. And instead of a hot pad she grabs a towel and starts to take the pan out.

"Watch out!" I warn, but too late. A foot away from the oven she flinches and drops the pan. It hits the oven door and turns over, spilling chicken breasts onto the floor. Grease splatters and hits Linda on her legs. She hops back, slips, and falls.

Now all the chicken is on the floor and Linda is sitting on three of the breasts. She scrambles up with big grease stains on her butt.

"Hurry," she says. "Get them up."

"They're ruined," I tell her.

"Nonsense. No one will ever know."

"You can't be serious."

"Just do it."

And so the show goes on. Linda scoops the chicken onto plates. My assistant, who has to serve the plates, watches as I try to salvage the three decimated entrees, which look more like veal chops now than chicken breasts. The sauce doesn't help much, since it's white wine and butter with capers. Who will be fooled by this? I'm in a panic, but all Linda says is "Damn, I lost a nail."

Out go the plates. Linda and I are glued to the door, listening. Everything sounds all right. And then it comes.

"Oh my God, what's this?"

"Goodness, Francine, it looks like part of some woman's fingernail."

—*Gene, 47, Tennessee*

● ● ● ● ● ● ● ● M Y BOSS FROM HELL AC-tually was my ex-boss when this happened. I worked as a teller at a bank for three years, and the branch manager was this guy named Arthur Woods. Arthur was married, but he was fooling around with one of the tellers, a woman named Yvette, and everybody knew it.

Now, I got a new job as a new-accounts clerk at another bank, so I quit working for Art. About six months go by and I'm sitting at my desk with a long line of customers waiting, because it's the start of the new school year and a lot of college students are opening accounts. The bank is full of people.

This woman walks in and I see her ask the security guard a question, then she stomps over to my desk. I can tell by the way she's walking that she means business, but I don't remember her face at all.

She stops in front of my desk and says in a real loud voice, "Are you Mitzi Waterman?"

I say yes.

"The same Mitzi Waterman who used to work at Third National over on Oak?"

I say yes again, but I can't place her from my old job either.

"I'm Florence Woods."

It takes me a minute, but then I say, "Arthur's wife?"

"Yes!" she says, like she just won a prize or something.

"What can I do for you?"

"You can stop sleeping with my husband, you slut!"

All I can do is stare at her for a second. I never dreamed of even holding Arthur's hand, let alone having an affair with him. "I'm sorry," I stutter, "but you must be mistaken. I haven't seen Arthur since I left Third National, and I have never been involved with him."

"Don't lie to me! He told me it was over when you quit, but I know you're still seeing him. You were with him this weekend at Sun River, weren't you? You better stop, missy, if you know what's good for you."

And she stomps away. The entire bank is staring at me, and the branch manager, a great lady named Lillian, comes over and has somebody else take care of new accounts. Lillian takes me into her office and asks me what's going on.

I tell her about Arthur and Yvette and that I never had an affair with him. Lillian knows I wasn't in Sun River this last weekend because I ran into her at the movies with my mother. I can tell she believes me, and she lets me go home.

On the way home I think somebody is following me, and I'm convinced that Mrs. Woods has hired a private detective. I think maybe I'm getting paranoid, but when I stop at the grocery store I notice this woman staring at me. Then I realize she's a customer at the bank and must have been there during the scene.

I try to call Mrs. Woods at home and explain again, but there's no answer.

That night I call my friend Rich at Third National and real casually ask him what's up. He tells me that Arthur and Yvette were on the rocks because Mrs. Woods found out he was seeing somebody, but they seem to have started up again because they went away together last weekend.

I call my parents but they're not home, so I turn on the radio. This is one of those call-in shows where a shrink gives personal advice. I think maybe I'll call in and ask her how I get out of this mess, when another woman comes on and I recognize her voice. It's Mrs. Woods.

She pours out this whole story about how her husband has been cheating on her with a woman he works with. She's in a motel room somewhere and she's sobbing and she sounds pathetic. I even feel a little sorry for her until I hear her tell the shrink about how she confronted the other woman today and how much better it makes her feel and how she wants to see this Mitzi suffer.

She said my name on the radio! I mean, everybody in town doesn't know me or anything, but all my friends know I work in a bank. This is so humiliating.

I try to call the show, but they go off the air as soon as the shrink tells Mrs. Woods that she needs some regular counseling. She also tells her it's better not to continue confronting this Mitzi, because who knows how she'll react. I'm glad to be off the hook, but now everyone in town suspects that I'm an unbalanced husband-stealer. I feel like I'm Joan Crawford in *The Women*.

That night I cry myself to sleep. In the morning I call Lillian at home and tell her I'm going to be late. Then I drive over to Third National before they open, and one of the tellers lets me in. Nobody says hello to me except Rich, and they all look away. I walk straight to Arthur's office and throw the door open.

Yvette's in there with him, and they look like they just saw a ghost.

"Heh, heh, Mitzi," Arthur says nervously. "How are you?"

"How am I? You scum, you told your wife I was screwing you. Yesterday she mortifies me in front of a bankful of people, and then she goes on the radio and tells the whole town. How the hell do you think I am, you lousy bastard?"

"Now, now, Mitzi, this will blow over. Florence is just a little emotional, that's all."

"Emotional! She's a basket case, and she's dangerous. I don't know how you could be so cruel to her or why she ever put up with you. But I don't have to take it. You call her right now and tell her the truth!"

Yvette gets up and tries to close the door so everyone else can't hear me screaming, but I give her a real nasty look and she sits back down.

"I can't call her," Arthur whines. "I don't know where she is."

"She's in a hotel, you idiot. Start calling!"

"Mitzi, I'm sure this is going to work out. Florence will get a little therapy—"

"I don't care what Florence gets, but either you get her on the phone or I'm going straight to a lawyer and suing you for every penny you've got!"

And he picks up the phone and makes one call, which means he knew where Florence was all the time. And he starts baby-talking her for a while, and he keeps doing it until I say "tell her" for the third time.

So he tells her, in this miserable, sniveling way, and I can hear her screaming though I'm standing ten feet away from the phone. I can only imagine how she must feel now, since she's just made a fool of herself twice. I really do feel sorry for this woman, despite the damage she's done in my life. I stand there until Arthur finally hangs up, and then I walk out.

My lawyer tells me it would be really hard to nail Arthur without nailing his wife for slander, too, so I never did sue. But Lillian, good old Lillian, also worked for Third National once, and she wrote a letter to an old friend of hers in the main office, and that woman called me and got my story. A week later Arthur and Yvette were out on the street.

—*Mitzi, 33, Massachusetts*

5

Hearts of Stone

Your father was just in an accident and he only has three hours to live? Sorry, but the Wallace project is due by lunch. You can have an hour off for the funeral, but only if you request it in writing, in triplicate. Wednesday? Oh, no, that won't work. The exterminator is coming and you have to check for roaches after he's gone. Don't worry, the headstone will be there forever. You can visit his grave on your lunch hour. But don't take more than an hour. It sets a bad example.

● ● ● ● ● ● ● ● ● ● I WAS NEGOTIATING AN OP-
tion for a parcel of land with
a real estate broker. One of our clients wanted it. So did two
other parties. The broker told me she would accept best offers
by noon on Tuesday.

I told my boss, Allen, the senior partner in the law firm. He
said, "See if you can talk her into a couple of rounds of bidding.
I hate best offers."

I talked to the broker and she said, "Okay, I'll do one round
so everybody gets a chance to put a bid in. Then I'll take the
best offer of the second round."

I didn't see the point, but Tuesday morning I put in the client's
first bid. It was a lousy bid, but at least we were in. At least we
were until the broker called and told me she'd accepted a bid
for three times what we'd bid. I told her those weren't the terms
we'd agreed on, but she said she'd taken the offer.

Allen hit the roof. "This is an absolute disaster. How could
you let this happen? This is thoroughly unprofessional. Why
aren't you paying attention? Why do you let people treat you
this way? Why do you let people walk all over you? If you'd
made her want to do business with you, she never would have
taken that offer! I trusted you with this deal. I can't believe you
let me down like this."

I tried to explain, but I couldn't get a word in edgewise. Besides, I was crying too hard. I went back to my office and cried for another couple of hours. All my colleagues filed through to express condolences. They'd all heard every word of Allen's explosion. I went home and had one brandy. For me, that was drowning my sorrows.

I got in early the next day. I hadn't done any work the previous afternoon. I had to catch up. And then the phone rang and the message display said the caller was Allen. I picked it up.

"Frances, I'm very sorry about what I said to you yesterday. I was way out of line and said some very hurtful things. The situation was not your fault, and I overreacted. I hope you can forgive me."

I think I stammered something out, and then I sat there for about an hour. I had all this rage and I didn't know what to do with it.

I started reading through a new lease on some office space for the same client. I discovered that it omitted an important clause which I had negotiated. I checked my notes and made sure I had covered it in the bargaining. I had. I called the lessor and advised him the clause needed to be inserted. He claimed it hadn't been negotiated. I told him it had. He said he couldn't agree to it, and if we wanted it, the deal was off.

I went to see Allen. Jackpot. "Jesus, Frances, aren't you even paying attention to this job? This place has to be your number-one priority. Nothing else can come first! How can I trust you on these deals when you're acting like a kid right out of law school? Maybe you'd like to just do research? Is that it?"

My office. Tears. Colleagues. Home. Brandy. The next morning, Allen on my voice mail: "Frances, forget about what I said yesterday. I was just out of sorts. Do what you can to straighten that stuff out. Break the deal if you have to."

Now I'm a wreck. Every time my phone rings, I jump. The day passes, and another. It's the weekend. Monday, one of our biggest clients announces at lunch with Allen and me that he's switching his business to another firm. They're our major competitor, and his son-in-law has just finished an internship there. He likes what he hears about them.

In the car on the way back from lunch: "You've let me down

again, Frances! Why aren't you getting these people to trust you, take you into their confidence! That's what building a practice is all about, trust! But how can anybody trust you when you're so scattered, when you're so withdrawn? What kind of lawyer can you expect to be? This is really approaching the *rankest* incompetence. I think you've got some kind of emotional problem, something's wrong with your head."

And he turns and looks me right in the eye, "Have you considered seeing a therapist?"

—Frances, 28, Arizona

• • • • • • • • **J**OSEPH WAS A REALLY GOOD friend of mine. I knew he had some personal problems, but I went to work for him anyway because the job was interesting.

What I didn't know was how he inflicted his personal anguish on everyone who worked for him. He was a classic passive-aggressive. He'd give you a job to do, stand over you for twenty minutes until you were finished, and then say, "That's not how you're supposed to do it."

Or he'd let you spend weeks working on a special project, staying late at the office, working weekends. And then, as soon as the books were closed he'd say, "How come you never put in for your taxis and meals? You know that if you work late you're entitled to a dinner and a cab ride home. Oh well, too late."

I'd been writhing in this agony for about six months when I finally gave in to an older problem and had foot surgery. I had an enormous cast, and of course I was supposed to stay off it for a while. But I'd timed the surgery for a Friday, so I had a weekend, a full week off, and then another weekend before I went back to work.

I had to take a taxi to work that week—I couldn't manage

the bus. All those steps! And Thursday was Passover, so I worked until about two o'clock, and then I hired a car to take me up to my mother's house. Fifty dollars I spent to get there, but I was going to relax all weekend, and my mother would pamper me.

About an hour after I got to my mother's, the phone rang. It was Joseph. "You know," he said, "you can't keep taking all this time off. If you don't come in to work tomorrow, you have to forfeit your paycheck."

I was speechless—for about a second—and then I said, "Joseph, you knew all week I was coming up to my mother's and I wouldn't be in on Friday. You could have told me this on Monday. You could have told me this today before I left. You know what you can do with that paycheck? You can shove it up your ass."

And I hung up the phone.

Monday, I went back in and there was my paycheck in my desk drawer. I was still staring at it when Joseph stuck his head in and said, "What are you doing here? You should be at home, getting some rest!"

What I needed was a sanatorium.

—Gina, 40, Ohio

● ● ● ● ● ● ● ● **M**Y MARRIAGE TO EDGAR had been a joke for nearly three years when I started seeing Luis. He was kind and attentive, very smart, and he wanted to have children, something Edgar did not. I would have asked for a divorce, but Edgar was quite intimidating and very concerned about his position as a hospital administrator. A divorce would cast a shadow on that, so I had to proceed carefully.

Luis and I were very discreet about meeting each other, often driving quite a way from home. We had gone to a restaurant down along the Ohio River, and at dinner that night he was very sweet. Between our entrees and the coffee I leaned over to kiss him.

There was a tremendous flash, and when my eyes adjusted, I saw that the man at the next table had jumped up and was running for the door with a camera. Luis chased him, but he got away.

I was terribly distraught, essentially in tears. I knew the man must have been a detective hired by Edgar. How could he not suspect? I went home and huddled in bed, waiting for a confrontation when Edgar came home from a hospital board meeting, but he simply crawled into bed and went to sleep, ignoring me as always.

I snuck out of the house the next morning before Edgar awoke and went to my office. I sell residential real estate. It's actually something I am quite tired of, but I kept my hand in because I knew that if I were to divorce Edgar I would need an income of my own.

On my chair was a large, glossy photograph of Luis and myself from the night before. I stepped forward to pick it up, and I heard a deep laugh behind me.

I knew before I even turned around that it was Nathan standing there. Of course he had to know. Luis never called me at home, only at the office; once or twice he had even dropped by, although the visits had been months apart. Nathan was a schemer; all his dealings were definitely not on the up-and-up. He was not the sort of man I would have associated with by choice, but his wife was a friend of my sister's, so he had been my first contact when I entered the business.

He stood there with a disgusting grin on his face. "Pretty, isn't it?" And he laughed again.

I tore the picture in two, but he only stated the obvious. "I've got the negative, you know. Can make as many copies as I want."

"You had no right," I fumed.

"Maybe, but what's done is done."

"What do you want?"

"I'll give you two choices. Either I take a double share out of your commission, or you give me a little of what you've been spreading around with that Cuban."

I almost vomited, but somehow I managed to say, "You burn in hell, Nathan Kidd," and I pushed past him and ran to my car. I drove for hours, not caring that I was missing appointments and possibly losing sales. But in the end, I knew what I had to do. I went to Edgar's office and told him the truth.

Perhaps I had seriously misjudged this man to whom I had been married for seven years. Edgar was shocked, of course, but he told me he would give me an uncontested divorce and that he realized we had grown apart and it was probably his fault.

Then he volunteered to punch Nathan Kidd in the nose. I declined, though I could tell he was quite willing. I'll always be perversely grateful that that horrible man gave my marriage its last brush with romance.

—*Helen, 46, Pennsylvania*

● ● ● ● ● ● ● ● ● I HADN'T TAKEN A VACA-tion in the two years since I'd started working for Greg—a real petty tyrant, the kind who wanted updates every day on a project and who forced you to redraft a whole set of mechanical plans because he decided a week after he'd opted for standard switches that there ought to be dimmers. It didn't matter what the client wanted. Greg knew best.

I was one of three people working on a set of plans for an expansion of the city library. I was supposed to be working on the heating and cooling systems. Two days before I was supposed to leave for Aspen, Greg made major changes in everything. A supporting wall had a new doorway inserted, and a large meeting room was carved into two rooms. This played havoc with everyone's designs, not just mine.

I told Greg I couldn't get the changes made in my designs before I left, especially since the new doorway was forcing the reorganization of stacks, and that wasn't even finished yet.

"Well, you'll just have to cancel your vacation."

Cancel it? I'd already moved my vacation twice because the work kept shifting around, and it was only going to get busier between now and April, when Aspen would be a total waste of time. My friend Carla would kill me if I backed out again.

"Greg," I said, "you promised me this vacation. I've already spent three hundred dollars on a nonrefundable ticket, and I bought a new pair of skis."

"Listen, babe, no vacation, okay? I have to have you here."

I pleaded, I begged, I even cried, but it was no use. Greg just told me to stop blubbering and get back to work. So, no vacation. It was ten months before I got to spend a week at Lake of the Ozarks. Big deal.

Carla had a great time in Aspen though. She even met a banker, and now they've got a kid. All I've got is my grindstone to keep me warm.

—*Leah, 31, Missouri*

• • • • • • • • HAVE YOU FINISHED RAKing those leaves yet, mister?"

"No sir."

"How about mowing that back lawn?"

"No sir."

"Well, why the hell not?"

"Because it's raining."

"That's not what I'm paying you for, buddy. Get moving."

It takes me about two hours to mow the back lawn because the grass is all wet and keeps gunking up the blades. It's a total waste to rake the lawn 'cause the wind is blowing and the rain keeps knocking down more leaves. It's practically nighttime by the time I go back into the joker's garage with the rake.

"All finished?"

"Yes sir."

And he hands me five dollars, and I say, "Thanks, Dad."

—*Randy, 12, Maine*

● ● ● ● ● ● ● ● **M**Y WIFE, NAOMI, HAD TO have surgery for the veins in her legs. Ever since her mother died during an operation, she's been scared of doctors and hospitals, but she finally gave in after our daughter talked her into it. But I had to promise to be with her before they took her in and to sit with her until she woke up. I wouldn't have had it any other way.

The problem was Don, my boss. The operation was supposed to be the week after Thanksgiving, and that's a real busy time in the electronics business. Lots of people buying presents and new cameras so they can take pictures of the baby. Don didn't want to give me the day off. I would have felt better taking a couple of days, since Naomi wasn't going to be getting around too good. So I thought one day wouldn't be a real problem for Don.

But he really busted my chops.

First off he said, "Forget it, Frank, you gotta be here."

I pointed out how I never even called in sick, so maybe he could just call this a sick day, but he said, "You call in sick that day, and you're fired."

I told him how worried Naomi was and how it was the right thing for a man to be there when his wife had an operation, but he just said, "Your wife's a baby. Nothin's gonna go wrong."

I kept after him, but he pointed at the door and said, "Fifty thousand people are gonna be in here and I need every sales-man I got. That means you, Frank."

So the day comes, and I go into the store. And at lunch I tell Frank that I gotta go, 'cause Naomi's at the hospital and the operation is at three o'clock. And he says, "You better come back from lunch, Frank. I mean it."

But I went to the hospital anyway, and everything came out just fine with Naomi's legs. I was sitting in her room afterward, waiting for her to wake up, and the phone rang, so I answered it.

And it's this bastard, Don. All he says is, "You're fired. I hope the bitch is a cripple."

—Frank, 60, Rhode Island

● ● ● ● ● ● ● **F**IVE YEARS I WAS THAT woman's secretary, and I showed up every day, and I did everything she told me, and she never had a complaint about anything I did.

Then I had an accident, and I broke my collarbone and my right arm. I had to go on medical leave for two months because those things take a while to heal, and I was supposed to take it easy—doctor's orders. I was in the hospital for a week at the start, and I never heard from her, not once.

Just before I was ready to go back to work, I called her and told her the doctor said I could start in a week and a half. All she said to me was, "That's nice, Marie. Call personnel and they'll set you up."

I didn't know exactly what she meant about me getting set up, but I called the woman in personnel, and she told me Bridgett had hired another woman to take my place! I wasn't going to be working for Her Highness anymore. In fact, they didn't even know what I'd be doing, but they'd find something for me.

I called my nephew, he's a lawyer. He told me they could do that to me. They just had to offer me "an equivalent position" and they couldn't cut my pay.

For the first couple of weeks I was back I just shuffled from one office to another, filling in for people who were sick or taking a vacation. And did Bridgett ever come around to see me or find out how I was doing? You better believe she didn't.

But finally they put me to work for a vice president, a real nice fellow, and I liked him. I'd see Bridgett walk past, and she'd just look at me and smile like I wasn't anybody. I was kind of getting over it when my new boss called me into his office. He told me the woman who Bridgett had hired to replace me had quit and Bridgett wanted me back!

I was never so mad in all my life, and I told him I'd quit before I went back to work for that cold fish. But he was real nice, and he told me he liked me and he would make sure I could stay where I was. And I did.

So a few weeks later I heard that Bridgett had hired a new secretary, and I saw her coming down the hall to introduce the secretary to the vice presidents. I guess she felt it was important for the vice presidents to know her secretary. It was more than she ever did for me.

She comes to our office and she takes this woman in to meet my boss and they come back out. They stop in front of my desk and she says, "Meredith, this is . . ."

She looks blank for a second, then she stares me right in the eye and says, "Excuse me, I've forgotten your name."

—*Marie, 47, Arkansas*

● ● ● ● ● ● ● ● ● CRAIG AND ME BOTH worked at the store before we got married, and Wanda, she didn't like that. She had this idea that people who worked together shouldn't see each other or date or anything. So when we got married she decided to get her revenge.

She wasn't the boss for either of us, not directly at least. I worked in cameras and Craig was in auto supply, and we each had a boss in our department. Wanda was the general manager for the whole store.

Before we got married Craig and me had almost the exact same schedule, except I worked Tuesday nights and he worked Thursdays. It was a good schedule. But the week after we got back from our honeymoon—we went to Tahoe—all of a sudden I was working all days and Craig was all nights. My boss, Wayne, he told me it was just because another girl needed to work Tuesday nights. But Jay, he was Craig's boss, he admitted that Wanda put him up to it.

I mean, here we were, just married and everything, and she was keepin' us apart. Then this woman, Patty Ann, who worked in women's clothes, she started spreading this rumor that Craig was foolin' around with Cindy in housewares. I knew that was a lie because Craig hated Cindy's guts, and she also worked the same shifts I did, so Craig didn't have a chance to see her any more than he could see me. Besides, everybody knew Patty Ann was a real brown noser and she'd do anything that Wanda told her.

Then one day I came back from lunch, and Wayne, he pulls me aside and tells me I'm bein' transferred to another store way over on the other side of town. And I told him I didn't want to work all the way out there, and he just said there was nothin' I could do about it 'cause they were short a person and we had too many. Which wasn't true that we had too many people.

So now I gotta drive an extra twenty minutes to get to work, and I hardly ever see Craig except on weekends. It just makes me so mad that that woman couldn't stand to see two people who love each other. I hope her husband is sleepin' with his secretary or somethin'.

—*Kim, 22, Arkansas*

● ● ● ● ● ● ● ● ● ● ● **I**T WAS THE MOST UNETH-ical job I've ever had. Six of us sat around in the early hours of the morning, calling people all over the country. We would feed them a line about calling "from the company that's been sending your magazines to you" and try to trick unsuspecting housewives into buying a huge package of magazines for five years at a time. The weekly payments were low, but "just $2.59" a week adds up to a lot of money over five years, especially when you could get better rates straight from the magazine.

I'd been on the job two days, trying to scrape tuition money together, and I hadn't made a sale. The boss, Ellie, decided to sit down next to me and show me how it was done. She was as big as a house, dressed in a floral tent, and she chain-smoked unfiltered Camels. But she had the smoothest voice you ever heard, and in half an hour she signed up three out of the five suckers she called.

"There," she cooed, "see how it's done?" And she shoved a photocopy of the Norfolk, Virginia, telephone listings for *R* in front of me and handed me the phone. She picked up another handset to listen in.

So I dialed. Mrs. Steven Randolph wasn't in, nor anybody at the William Randolph house. But I got Mrs. David Random on the first ring. I started my spiel, and the lady cut right in. She didn't subscribe to any magazines, she didn't want any magazines, and what was I doing—

Click. Jab. Ellie had cut the connection and stuck a ballpoint pen into my side simultaneously. "Don't waste your time with those bastards!" she hissed. I looked at my shirt, expecting blood.

I made three more calls, getting jabbed all the while as I flubbed the script. My heart wasn't in this job, but I expected to see my guts all over the floor any minute. Ellie was losing patience. "You've got to make them trust you. For chrissake, be a salesman!"

My next call was Mrs. Alice Raney, and I knew already that women who listed themselves that way were often elderly widows. Mrs. Raney was delighted to hear from me. She was so happy with her magazines; they kept her company. My heart had sunk so low that it was somewhere around my ankles, but I knew I could sell this woman a lifetime supply of magazines.

"Close the deal!" Ellie snapped. *Jah. Jah.* "You've got her."

Then Mrs. Raney told me she hoped she could pay her bill just once a month, since that's when she got her Social Security check. I disconnected.

I waited for the fatal jab, but Ellie slapped me instead—so hard that I fell off my chair. "Idiot!" she was screaming, even as she lunged for the list of phone numbers and started calling Mrs. Raney back.

For a brief moment I had visions of strangling her with the phone cord. Instead I grabbed the list of numbers, hit the disconnect again, and ran out the door.

When I got home, I sent a letter to the Better Business Bureau.

—Larry, 25, Minnesota

● ● ● ● ● ● ● ● **P**ETE IS MY TWIN BROTHER, and after we graduated from high school, we both started working full-time at the same hardware store. We were gonna go to college together, and we got an apartment together, too.

For some reason, old Mr. Bonham didn't like Pete, and he was always makin' him do things like count the nails in a bin or somethin' else that was real stupid. Pete figured out pretty quick that Mr. Bonham wanted him to quit, but he didn't let on. We'd always done everything together, so he put up with it.

So school starts, and we pay our tuition for the term and we're pretty much flat broke, but since we're workin' during the day and our classes are mostly at night, we aren't gonna have much of a chance to spend anything anyway, so we're happy. Then old Mr. Bonham calls us aside when we come in one day, and he tells us they've got too many salespeople, and he's gonna have to let one of us go. And he wants us to pick which one is gonna be fired.

Well, that's a pretty goddamned lousy thing to do in the first place, what with us just havin' paid our tuition, and he knows about that. Plus, me an' Pete had always worked together, and he knew that, too. But for him to ask us to pick which one of us is gonna get fired, that's just downright mean, no two ways about it.

So I look at Pete for a second, and then I say, "I guess I'll go."

And Mr. Bonham starts to stammer sort of, and then he has the balls to say, "I'd rather it was Pete."

Hey, he gave us the choice. And if he was low-down enough to be such a weasel about it in the first place, he better have the guts to stick by what we chose. So I tell him it's got to be Pete who stays.

Then he says Pete is a lazy worker and that he doesn't know enough about the stock, which is a damn lie, because I don't know any more about pipes and pulleys than Pete does. So finally he tells us we're both fired.

And because he fired both of us, the people at unemployment say he has to pay benefits for both of us. I bet he probably wanted to pick just one of us.

—*Paul, 25, Nebraska*

● ● ● ● ● ● ● ● ● **I** WENT TO ALASKA TO GET rich. Or at least pay for a year of college. The work in the salmon canneries was long, but mostly it wasn't hard. You just stood in place all day, working the "slime line," which is what they called cleaning the catch.

The problem was that the supervisor was my ex-girlfriend, Kathy. Kathy had done this for three years now, and I'd learned from her about how much money you could make. We'd even gone up there together, although we'd pretended we didn't know each other so there wouldn't be any problem with me working for her.

On my fourth day in Alaska, Kathy became my ex-girlfriend. We had some big fight about getting engaged—I only remember that I wasn't ready yet. She was.

The first week was all right. I just slimed away for about thirteen hours a day. Kathy seemed to be flirting a lot with other guys, but I pretended not to notice, since I figured it was all for my benefit. On Saturday we ran out of fish about two in the afternoon. Most of the people went back to their tents, but I volunteered for a cleaning detail. After all, I was here for money. What a fool I was!

Kathy assigned me to cleaning out the big hopper where the fish went after they'd been slimed and before they were chopped up and canned. I had to climb a big ladder to the top, then swing over and lower myself down to the bottom, which was funnel-shaped. I was handed a big plastic brush and a hose, and I started scrubbing. There were scales and crusty fish guts all over the hopper, and I had to stand funny since there was no flat floor.

Pretty soon my legs were damn tired and I wanted a rest on a regular floor, so I grabbed the top of the hopper to haul myself out. When I got my head over the rim, I could see that the ladder was gone.

I called to one of the guys to bring it over, but Kathy stopped him and said, "Are you done yet?"

I told her I wasn't.

"You can't come out till you're done."

"You've got to be joking."

"When you start something, buster, you'd better finish it."

I got that message loud and clear. I went back to work, and about an hour later all the gunk was loosened up and washed out the bottom of the hopper. I hauled myself up to the top again.

"Hey, I'm through. Let me out of here."

"Just a minute," Kathy yelled. "I'm going to inspect your work." And about five minutes later she finally dragged a ladder over and climbed up. She was carrying a bucket.

"Look," I said. "Spick-and-span."

"No," she replied. "You missed a spot."

"Where?" I accused.

"Here," she yelled, and she dumped a bucket of fish guts over my head.

—Scot, 22, Washington

O KAY, SO YOU READ MY buddy Scot's story about Alaska. That was nothing compared to what I went through.

I went up there with Scot and Kathy, but because my girlfriend wasn't a supervisor I didn't get hired right away. I sat around for three weeks waiting for an opening at one of the canneries. One day I'm at the employment office, and this Japanese guy comes along and says he's hiring, and everybody crowds around him.

The twist is that it isn't local. He's got a processing plant in Bristol Bay, which is about three hundred miles west. But instead of living in a tent, they have dormitories, all your food is provided, and there are showers. And the pay is almost twice as much as anybody is making here in town.

"Very modern," says this Mr. Ichigawa. "Good place to work."

Anybody who wants to go should be at the airport at dawn the next day.

So Kathy tells me the Japanese have been opening all these new processing plants and she saw one last year that looked like a dairy, it was so clean and shiny. And boy, I'm tired of sleeping in a sleeping bag and eating Pop-Tarts for breakfast, lunch and dinner. I can't even remember the last time I took a shower. It sounds great to me.

So we get on this plane and we start to fly. For a long time we're out over water, Bristol Bay, which is pretty enormous. And after a while we see these buildings along the shore, and we come in for a landing on this tiny little strip.

Even before we hit the ground I can tell this isn't any modern processing plant. It looks like the Russians built it when they owned Alaska. And there is absolutely nothing around. No town, not even a few houses. It looks like a prison camp out in the middle of nowhere. Which it was.

The dormitories were Quonset huts and the bunks just some metal springs with no mattresses, so I still end up sleeping in my bag. When we turn on the water in the showers, it comes out a deep rust color and it never gets hot. Believe me, ground water in Alaska is pretty friggin' cold.

Right away they put us to work, even though it's lunchtime and we haven't been fed. Mr. Ichigawa disappears, and he's replaced by this guy named Oscar who looks like he chews nails and shits tacks. I take a place on the canning line, where I'm laying the fish out on the conveyor belt. I keep getting these things that don't look like salmon to me. One of them actually looks like some kind of a baby shark, but who can tell with the head and tail and fins cut off.

I drop these strange looking things into a bucket, and Oscar comes along and he yells, "What the hell do you think you're doing?"

"Those aren't salmon."

"I don't care what the hell you think they are, buddy, stick 'em in there."

So now you know why I won't eat canned salmon, because I saw what went into those machines.

Anyway, we work about five hours without a break, and I ask the guy next to me what time's dinner. "Whenever we finish," he yells back over the noise.

"How long?" I yell.

"Probably another five or six hours," he shouts back.

I'm about to ask him another amazing question, when all of a sudden Oscar's in my face. "You got a problem, buddy?" His breath smells like he gargles with fish heads.

"How about a break?" I shout.

"You son of a bitch, you'll get a break when I tell you you'll get a break."

So another five hours drags by, and I mean drags, because this stuff is real monotonous. I mean, if you stuck one fish on a belt, you've stuck a thousand fish on a belt. Finally we're done, and I follow everybody else to the mess hall.

Which is a total joke. They serve us Kool-Aid and oatmeal, which tastes like it was made when Eisenhower was president. We all go back to the barracks and collapse, and about five o'clock in the morning, Oscar comes through banging a pipe against a bucket and tells us we have to start working in ten minutes. There isn't even enough time for all of us to use the bathroom.

So another two days go by like this. We get two meals a day, no breakfast, and once lunch is just applesauce and rusty water, which tells me the Kool-Aid was also probably made with rusty water.

Finally, I tell Oscar that I'm quitting and I want out.

He looks at me, and laughs, and says, "Fine, start walking. You'll probably hit Ugashik about noon tomorrow. It's about thirty miles. Watch out for the bears."

—Kyle, 21, Washington

6

Tales of the One-Eyed Monster

Anita Hill? Who's she? Come over here, my dear, and let me smell that lovely perfume you're wearing. You're not wearing any? My, what an attractive natural scent you have. It's especially alluring here behind your ear, and your skin is so smooth, it reminds me of a baby's bottom. Have I ever told you how exciting redheads are? It's that feisty temper that's so stimulating.

● ● ● ● ● ● ● ● ● ● I KNEW NANCY FROM grade school. She was a bitch then and she was still a bitch when we grew up. It really burned me when she got promoted to manager at the Dairy Queen. But I kept my mouth shut.

Thursdays were okay, though, 'cause that was when I worked the night shift, and I didn't have to listen to her slappin' her fat mouth. I guess I worked about six months without ever suspectin' somethin' was up, all the time thinkin' Thursday was the sweetest night of the week.

One night, though, and it was a Thursday, some drunk hit the telephone pole outside and we lost our electricity. I called Mrs. Parker, who owned the place, and I told her we were just gonna close up. She said fine. This was about eight o'clock, three hours before we usually closed.

So I pull into my street, and there's Nancy's car in front of my house. The power was still on—I could see it in the streetlight. There weren't any lights on in the house, but that was okay because Thursday was my husband, Dale's, bowling league. I didn't go into the driveway because if that woman was sneakin' around my house, I wanted to know why. So I parked about three houses away, and I snuck up to her car. It was empty, and the engine wasn't warm, so I knew she'd been here a while.

I walked around the outside of the house, but I didn't see her, so I went in through the back door into the kitchen. There were a couple of empty Buds on the counter, and I thought, damn, if that woman is sneakin' into my house and drinkin' my beer, I'm gonna pull her hair out.

There wasn't anybody in the living room, but when I stood in the hall I could hear noises coming from the bedroom. I walked straight down the hall and threw open the door.

And there she was, in bed with my husband!

—*Lonnie, 23, Oklahoma*

● ● ● ● ● ● ● ● ● **I** HATE OPENING BECAUSE I have to be at the restaurant at six in the morning to work the drive-through window. One morning I wake up late, and I race down there. I make it with about five minutes to spare, and as I run in the back door, I see Lou, the manager, who's such a creep.

"Hurry up," he snarls as I dash into the bathroom and start changing into my uniform. I usually come to work with my uniform on already, but today I'm in such a rush.

I drop my jeans and step out of them, and as I bend over to pick them up, I feel a draft on the back of my legs. I look around, and the door is open, just a crack, and I can see an eye. And I scream, "Lou, you bastard." He's the only other person in the restaurant at this hour, and he's about to be all alone again.

—*Donna, 18, Nebraska*

● ● ● ● ● ● ● ● ●**V**INCE WAS VERY ATTRACT-
ed to me. He lingered over
my desk, he touched my hand whenever he passed me something, and he was always inviting me out for coffee at lunch or
for a drink after work.

I made all kinds of obvious comments to let him know that I
already had a boyfriend and that I wasn't interested, but he just
didn't get it. I couldn't imagine fooling around with someone I
worked for anyway, but Vince had trouble bathing regularly,
and there was always stuff stuck to his shirt and cuffs. I didn't
want to know what it was.

Once, we had some T-shirts printed up to promote a show
we were running in the gallery. When they arrived, he took one
out of the box and said, "Here, try it on."

I sighed and headed for the washroom. "No, no. There's no
one here right now. Just take your shirt off and put it on."

I threw the shirt back at him and said, "I'm sure it fits."

So, knowing all this, why did I agree to go to an opening with
him way out in Lake Park? Well, I was interested in the show,
and I had the use of my sister's car, so I knew I wouldn't be
dependent on the trains to get back into the city.

But as soon as we got there, I knew it was going to be a long
night. Vince clung to me. He introduced me to all his friends
with a knowing look, and they all leered back. I just knew he'd
been telling them his fantasies about me as if they were fact.

People started filing out around nine-thirty, and I made noises
about having to get home. No, no, he insisted, I had to drop by
his house and have a drink. A few of his friends would be coming by, and one of them was the owner of another gallery that
I was really interested in working at.

I would dash into the lion's jaws if that meant I could escape
his den. Of course none of his friends dropped by. I politely
sipped my brandy until I announced I really had to be going. It
was nearly eleven.

"Oh, I've got plenty of room here. You don't need to make

that long drive back into the city," Vince protested. He sat down on the couch next to me. "Besides, the cats will make room for both of us in the bed."

He gave me what must have been a 20,000-watt leer and set his hand on my thigh. I jumped and kept on going straight for the door.

"Mitch, Mitch, wait, wait." He chased me down the steps and across the lawn. He tried to stand in front of the car door, but I pushed him aside, jumped in and drove off. On the way out of his driveway I hit his mailbox and knocked it over. It was an accident. Honest.

It took me exactly four days to get the job at that other gallery. Now I'm a partner there. Thanks, Vince.

—*Mitch, 32, Illinois*

● ● ● ● ● ● ● ● ● I WAS HALFWAY AROUND the world. I was supposed to be assisting in community work projects in India's villages, and my "boss" there was an official in the Ministry of Development. I'd met him at the airport in New Delhi, and his hug of greeting had gone on awfully long.

A day later we'd flown to a smaller city on the western coast, where we would spend the night and then drive out to a development center about a hundred miles away.

Indian society was very polite, but Mr. Khan was taking it a bit far. "You are a very remarkable woman, Miss Lesh, so intelligent, and so very beautiful."

We stayed that first night in a guest house at the state university. It had ten rooms, but we were the only two occupants. He insisted on carrying my bag to my room, and he lingered until I pretended to have stomach cramps.

At dinner we were joined by several other officials and some Americans doing research. There was lots of small talk, very polite, but Mr. Khan kept interjecting things like, "You have such beautiful ruby red lips." He sat next to me, and I had to keep my legs tucked under my chair to avoid those oh, so casual brushes with his roving limbs.

At one point he excused himself and went back to his room. I relaxed a little, though I still didn't know how I was going to work with this guy for three months.

Forget three months. I had ten minutes until he was back. He was dressed in this immaculately pressed linen outfit covered with expensive embroidery, all loose and flowing. I could only think of pajamas.

I kept talking and talking until the others began drifting away. Finally, we were the only ones left in the guest house.

Mr. Khan followed me to my room. I didn't open the door.

"Again, let me tell you how so very beautiful you are." He stepped closer.

"Good night, Mr. Khan," I said firmly.

"I am hoping that we may talk some more."

"I'm sorry, but I am very tired."

And then suddenly his hands are on my arms and he's pulling me closer and his lips are coming up to mine. I twist and manage to grab the doorknob, which means that he plants a wet one on my chin instead of my mouth.

"Back off!" I shout, kicking him on the shin.

He stumbles back, and I dart inside. He's fast, though, and I have to slam the door on his foot twice before he yanks it away. I throw the lock and collapse on the bed.

I really want a drink, but I'm not going back downstairs to get one, so I change and crawl into bed. I'm too wound up to sleep, despite all my travel in the last few days. I don't know how long I'm lying there before I hear a scrape at the window.

There he is—on a ladder, for God's sake, though it's only about five feet to the ground. I can hear him saying something about how sorry he is, but if he's so sorry, why isn't he talking to me through the door instead of trying to climb in my window?

Well, I saw this in a movie once, and it seems cruel, but I'm in no mood for charity. I pull the window up.

"Oh, Miss Lesh, I am so terribly, terribly—"

It isn't as easy to push the ladder away as I thought it would be. He's heavy, and once he sees what I'm doing, he grabs my arms again.

So I spit in his face. This startles him enough that he lets go with one hand, and I use my right arm to push him sideways instead of backwards. Now he starts to fall, but he's still got hold of my left arm with both hands now. The last thing I want is to end up in a heap on the ground with Romeo.

Call it dirty pool, but I slam him a good one on the ear with the palm of my hand. The ladder is shifting away from him now, but he's still got my arm. I lean back, and bring the window down hard. One arm lets go immediately, and then the other, as the ladder falls to the right and down he goes to the left. Goodbye, Dr. Strangelove.

In the morning I flew back to Delhi. It only took two days to get a flight to the States.

—Julie, 29, Missouri

● ● ● ● ● ● ● ● ● **M**Y BROTHER, JAKE, WORK-ed for Mr. Iverson when he was in high school, but when he graduated and went off to college, he told me I should ask for the job.

Jake did all Mr. Iverson's yard work. The Iversons had a great big house down on the lake, with lots of lawns and trees. The lawn had to be mowed twice a week, and Mr. Iverson paid Jake five dollars an hour.

I went to see Mr. Iverson one afternoon, and he laughed at me and said, "It's too much work for a girl." That made me pretty mad, but my dad told me if I thought I could do the work I ought to at least try it. So I went back and talked him into it, even though he kept laughing at me. But he told me he'd only pay me three dollars an hour, which is what Jake got when he started. I thought that was pretty unfair, but I gave in because I wanted the money.

Mr. Iverson was very particular about his lawn. He took me outside and showed me where it had just been mowed. "You see that pattern the mower makes? You have to mow the lawn in that same pattern every time. The grass is used to it, and if you mow it another way, you'll ruin my lawn."

So I came back three days later and I got the mower out of the shed. For a rich guy Mr. Iverson had a pretty cheap lawn mower. The one we had at home had a motor that pushed it forward, but this one hardly moved at all unless you leaned into it. I started near the house, following the dumb pattern, and Mr. Iverson came running out.

"No, no, you're going in the wrong direction. The grass has to be cut going the other way."

I hauled the mower around and I started mowing in the opposite direction. The catcher bag was pretty small, and after I'd carried it out back to the mulch pile for the third time, I got the wheel barrow and decided to fill it up with a couple of bagfuls and then take it to the mulch pile.

Mr. Iverson came running out again. "Don't take that wheel barrow onto the grass. It'll make a rut in the lawn."

I had to go back to the old way. It took me about three hours to do most of the lawn, and all I had left was the part where the lawn sloped down to the lake. This was when I noticed that the pattern didn't go across the slope, it went up and down. The lawn practically ran into the lake. There was just a little stone wall about a foot wide at the bottom, and it stuck up about three inches over the grass.

I started down there, and I pushed the mower up to the top and turned around. I saw that Mr. Iverson had come outside again, and he was just standing on the patio with his arms folded, watching me. When I went back down the hill I had to pull the mower back really hard to keep it from running away from me. I looked at Mr. Iverson, and he was laughing.

Each time I pushed that mower up the hill, it got harder, and pretty soon I was almost digging my heels in on the way down. Mr. Iverson had gotten himself an iced tea now, and he was sitting in a lawn chair with a big smile on his face.

I pushed that mower up the hill for about the hundredth time, and Mr. Iverson yelled to me, "Had enough yet? I told you it was too hard for a girl."

Now that really made me mad. I swung the mower around real fast and started down the hill, but my foot slipped and my legs went out from under me. I lost hold of the mower, and it took off like a bat out of hell. It went straight down the hill, hit the little wall, and arced up like a skier does out of a jump. It made a big splash before it sank into the lake.

Boy, was Mr. Iverson mad. He came running down the hill past me, screaming and yelling and waving his arms. He looked like he was going to jump in the lake after the mower for a minute. Then he turned and ran back up to me and really laid into me.

He told me I was going to have to pay for a new mower and he wasn't paying me for the work I'd done, that I'd made a big hole in his lawn where my foot slipped, and that he never should have hired a stupid girl to mow his lawn.

I didn't care what he said 'cause I'd sprained my ankle when I slipped. He wouldn't even let me call my mom to come drive me home, so I had to limp back to my house pushing my bicycle. I thought about leaving the bike so it would be easier to walk, but I was afraid Mr. Iverson would throw it in the lake just to get even.

I didn't have to pay for a new mower, though. Jake told my mom that Mr. Iverson had two lawn mowers, the cruddy old one that I'd used and a fancy new one with power drive he kept in the garage like it was a car. That was the mower Jake always used.

So Mr. Iverson had done that to me on purpose, and it was all his fault that his mower was under six feet of water. My mom said that instead of me having to pay for a mower, Mr. Iverson ought to pay my doctor's bill. But he didn't.

—*Kristin, 16, Vermont*

● ● ● ● ● ● ● ● ● ● IT GETS PRETTY LONELY at an airport at night when you're in an office in a hangar a long way from a terminal. That's why I didn't mind when Al would hang around after the day shift was done and keep me company.

He was the regional manager for this air freight company that I worked for, and he was supposed to be done at three o'clock when I came on. But he'd stay, sometimes for a couple of hours, and we'd talk, and maybe flirt a little, but it seemed pretty harmless, since we were both married.

There wasn't much outgoing traffic from our town; most of the company's business was incoming in the mornings. So a lot of times I didn't have much to do. Al would sometimes drop in later in the evening, saying he'd forgotten something in the office, and he'd stick around and we'd talk some more.

So one night he comes in, and he asks me to come into his office. I thought maybe something was wrong, because I knew business was slow.

He shuts the door, then he unzips his pants, pulls out his dick, and says, "Masturbate me."

Right. The only thing I could do was laugh.

—*Lydia, 23, Kansas*

7

Bad Habits

Miss Manners turns tail and runs from these folks. They don't see anything wrong with what they're doing, and why should they? It's only natural. In fact, everybody does it. They just won't admit it because they've got hang-ups. Don't be so uptight. Stick around and loosen up a bit. It's better to give in to that itch than to fight it. Otherwise, you'll give yourself a complex.

● ● ● ● ● ● ● ● W E ALL SUFFERED FROM the fact that Hank was crude. As station manager, he held everybody at our little oldies radio outfit in complete thrall; we all wondered what he'd do next.

Once he started picking his nose in a meeting with a prospective advertising client—a client who will now always remain a *prospective* advertiser. At the company Christmas party one year he forced the receptionist to slow dance with him, and planted his big greasy hand right on her butt in front of about twenty people. When the afternoon deejay's mother died, Hank started asking her if all her jewelry was stuff her mother had left her and tried to give her advice about cutting her sister out of the will.

His crudeness was even worse when he drank, which was daily. He'd often come back from a liquid lunch, go into his office and shut the door. We usually heard him snoring about five minutes later.

To make it all worse, he was a dictator. No one could talk anything over with Hank. You did it his way, or you were gone.

All this had an inevitable effect on morale, and as a result our ratings slipped. The day word came that we'd dropped below the local college station in the ratings, Hank left for lunch about ten-thirty, and he didn't come back until three.

I was in the lobby, chatting up the new receptionist, when the elevator doors opened. Hank was in there, and he had his fists up, trying to punch some guy. The other guy just gave Hank a shove, and Hank stumbled out of the elevator and landed on the floor. He struggled to get up, and it was pretty obvious that two arms and two legs were more than he could think about at once. Neither of us tried to help him.

He finally managed to get to his feet, and he swung around with his fists up again, but the elevator was gone. He lurched around and looked at us, but by the way he squinted, I didn't think he could really see us, let alone recognize us.

He stumbled forward, then lurched again and wove his way to the wall and just stood there a moment, leaning on it for support. He took two steps forward and walked into a big plant. He kicked the pot with the side of his foot and just stood there again, swaying.

Then, real deliberately, he reached down and unzipped his fly. He pulled his dick out and started pissing on the plant!

—*Grant, 42, Colorado*

● ● ● ● ● ● ● ● ● **I** CAN'T TELL YOU WHERE this happened, because it was a small town and a lot of the people involved still live there.

I was hired to accompany the local high school choir for the year. I went in for an hour during school, and sometimes I came back after school was out for extra rehearsals. The man who hired me was the choir director, a guy just out of college who thought he was some kind of hippie holdover. Lots of feel-good talk with the students about how he wanted to be their friend, how they should call him Ernie instead of Mr. Lambert, that kind of thing.

His wife, Shelley, didn't seem to have anything better to do than hang around during the after-school practices, so I saw a lot of her, too. She was just like him, lots of Stevie Nicks-style skirts. I think she was stoned a lot.

The biggest problem was that Ernie wanted to be more than friends with some of the girls. It was pretty obvious. He'd stand behind them, trying to get them to use their diaphragms when they sang, pulling on their stomachs when their notes started to waver. I'd seen this technique used before, but Ernie would stand behind these girls forever, with his arms around them through a whole cantata.

And Shelley didn't seem to mind a bit. In fact, she was awful friendly with a couple of the boys.

All this came to a head when we went on tour. We headed south from the town, singing mostly in churches and at a few other schools. The first couple of nights we were put up in homes, but on the third night we got to stay in a church, just rolling out the sleeping bags we'd brought along.

The girls were in the big community room on the main floor, and the boys were divided up into Sunday-school rooms. Shelley and I were the chaperons for the girls, and Ernie was supposed to watch the boys.

Shelley wandered off while the girls were rolling their sleeping bags out, but I didn't pay much attention because it was already pretty clear that she didn't take this supervising business very seriously. There wasn't much to it, actually—just make sure you had as many heads as names and that nobody was smoking.

But I counted twice, and I came up a girl short. I knew who it was: Danielle, one of Ernie's favorites. I moaned in my head and went looking.

I knocked on a couple of the Sunday-school rooms, but the guys were all there, only I couldn't find Ernie either. Now I was pretty worried. I started checking other rooms and finally the only place left was the pastor's office. I knocked, and I didn't get any answer, so I opened the door and stuck my head in.

Well, talk about killing two birds with one stone. There was Ernie, all right. Danielle, too. They still had their clothes on, but he was lying on top of her on the couch and the position of his hands made his intentions pretty clear.

He jumped up off her like he'd been stuck with a pin.

"What the hell do you want?" he yelled.

"Danielle was missing. I was worried when I couldn't find her. I'm glad to know she's in safe hands." It was mean of me to say that, especially to Danielle, but they both knew what they'd been doing.

"Well, you found her," Ernie said.

"Great," I replied. "Now I just have to find Shelley."

"What?"

"I've looked all over, and I can't find her either."

Ernie barreled out of the room and started running down the hall, opening all the doors. I knew she wasn't there, because I'd looked, but I followed him anyway. We didn't turn her up, but when we checked on one of the boy's rooms, one of them said, "Where's Mike?"

Ho ho! Mike was one of Shelley's favorites, and now I knew what Ernie was so excited about. He kept tearing around and finally we went out into the parking lot and started checking cars. Ernie made a lot of noise. Obviously, we weren't sneaking up on anybody.

We found them in our bus, hiding under a couple of seats. The bus reeked of pot, and when Ernie dragged Mike out, his shirt was misbuttoned and hanging out of his pants, which is what you'd expect from a kid who had to put his clothes back on lying on the floor of a bus half-stoned.

Ernie started shaking Mike, yelling, "You stay the hell away from my wife!" He drew back his fist, but Shelley grabbed it and the three of them were all struggling there in the aisle.

"You bitch!" Ernie yelled at Shelley.

"You pig!" she called him.

I didn't know what to do, so I started yelling "stop it" at the top of my lungs, and that got through to them.

"I can't believe this! The two of you are screwing the students and you get caught and all you can do is yell at each other? Mike, get out of here and go to bed right now!"

He climbed over a couple of seats and was out the door pronto.

"Listen," I said. "This is it. If you think I'm not reporting both of you when we get back, you've got another think coming. I can't believe you'd abuse these kids this way. It's disgusting. In fact, it's probably rape!"

"Hey," Ernie started to say, "Danielle is eight—"

"Shut up!" I screamed. "The two of you can just stay out here all night. I don't want you near those kids again unless it's absolutely necessary."

So I left them there and I rolled out my sleeping bag in front of the only church door that wasn't locked from the inside, and they spent the night in the bus.

Ernie quit as soon as we got home, but I reported them anyway. Danielle's parents sued the school, and I even got offered Ernie's job, but I turned it down. It seemed like the right time to get out of town.

—*Patty, 29, now a resident of North Dakota*

• • • • • • • • I DIDN'T ACTUALLY GO TO work for this guy, so maybe he doesn't count as a boss from hell. More like an interview from hell.

He's actually a friend of my father's, which is a strike against him to begin with, because I don't want my old man getting a day-to-day update on my job. But he is a sports agent, which is exactly what I want to do, so I think maybe it's worth a chance.

His secretary shows me in and he starts asking questions, but I have a hard time listening because he's taken a paper clip and unfolded it and is using it to drag big, honking gobs of wax out of his ear. Whenever he gets one, he sort of looks it over like it was a space alien, then he takes it and starts rubbing it between his fingers until it disappears. When that happens, he kind of rubs his hand on the desk, like he's polishing it with the wax.

After a while, he's mined his ears pretty good and he isn't coming up with anything more. So he straightens the paper clip out and starts using it to pick his teeth. It's really gross, because I can tell that a couple of times he's loosened some tasty morsel. While I tell him about how I've studied all kinds of sports contract-law, he digs out something about the size of a barge on the end of the clip, takes it off, studies it too, and then pops it back in and chews it.

Eventually he loses interest in his mouth and just fidgets for a few minutes. Then he bends over, so that I can barely see his eyes over the top of his desk. When he straightens up, he's got a shoe in one hand. He swings his leg around and puts his foot on top of the desk. There's a big hole in the bottom of his sock, which draws my attention like a bull's-eye. But he pulls the sock off, too, and he crosses his leg so his foot is in his lap.

He picks up the trusty paper clip again and goes after his toe jam, scraping it off onto the edge of the desk. All the time he's still asking me questions, but I'm really only mumbling my answers.

My final, real clue that maybe I don't want to work for this guy comes when he licks his finger, presses it down on top of the mountain of toe jam—and sticks it in his mouth.

—*David, 28, Maryland*

● ● ● ● ● ● ● ● ● WHEN I WAS A STUDENT I thought Dr. Kimball was wonderful, even if she seemed a little eccentric. I took the job as her secretary after I graduated because it let me stay around the college where my friends were, and I wasn't certain exactly what I was going to do with my degree in art history.

Dr. Kimball was the Dean of Women, and she had a very distinguished past. Her background was in physics, and she'd had something to do with the Manhattan Project. Before coming to the college she'd served on the boards of several prestigious scientific foundations. In the late 1950s these were impressive credentials for anyone to have but especially unusual in a woman.

But the first clue I had that something was a little amiss was at a reception for incoming students. On her name tag she wrote "Docter Kimball." I covered for that one by persuading her that her position ought to be on the name tag as well and just wrote a new one for "Dr. Kimball."

It didn't get any better. She started "correcting" the spelling in the letters I typed with some truly creative combinations. I had to send out letters with words like "particuler" and "great-full" in them because Dr. Kimball was certain that was the correct spelling, and she wouldn't be bothered with a dictionary. Every time she found one of my "mistakes," she'd call me in and give me a long lecture about sloppiness.

I mentioned that I'd thought Dr. Kimball was wonderful when I was a student. I think the thing that most endeared her to the students was that she seemed completely oblivious to the issue of gentility, which was something a dean of women was supposed to browbeat into her students. In fact, everyone learned not to walk too closely behind her when she was crossing the campus, because all of a sudden she would turn her head over her shoulder and spit. She never noticed if anyone was standing there. She just spit. Fortunately, she did not do this indoors.

Still, Dr. Kimball was very popular on campus. One day I learned that a group of her admirers had decided she would make a fantastic contestant on one of the game shows aired live from New York City, which was only half an hour away. Her wit and her strong character would make her appearance amusing, and everyone in the country would think great things about our school. They planned to "kidnap" Dr. Kimball and take her to New York, where she would be a walk-on contestant.

After six months working closely with Dr. Kimball, I knew otherwise. Not only was she rather scattered, but she did not take well to being told she was wrong. She was quite proud.

I don't know if this silly scheme would ever have worked out. I can't imagine what Dr. Kimball would have to say about being "kidnapped" in the first place. But it was clear that if her admirers tried to carry it out, there would be plenty of trouble.

So I went to the Dean of Men, who was a good friend of Dr. Kimball, and he was just as shocked as I was. He and I spent the rest of the afternoon chasing down the conspirators and talking them out of it.

Well, Dr. Kimball was in a pretty snit when I finally came back to the office. She gave me the "sloppiness" lecture for the millionth time, only with different adverbs and adjectives substituted, and told me she simply couldn't put up with such irresponsibility, though I'm sure she would have spelled it differently. She told me I was fired.

I broke down and told her what I'd been doing, and she launched into another lecture about lying. She didn't believe a word I'd said.

It was too late to get the Dean of Men to vouch for me because he'd gone home. He did speak up for me the next day, but it was too late and Dr. Kimball wouldn't be convinced. I was out of a job.

So I learned my lesson right then and there. When you're picking someone to work for, stay away from the charming, irrepressible types, because they'll get you every time.

—*Doreen, 57, New Hampshire*

ONCE UPON A TIME, A VERY long time ago, Bill had worked in Hollywood. I'm not even sure what he did, because as much as he talked about it, he never mentioned work, just names.

Now he owned an antiques store, and I was one of two employees. The store made outrageous sums of money on a single sale, so it didn't matter if nobody came in for hours at a time. And during those long dry spells, Bill would regale us with tidbits.

He'd had lunch dozens of times with Orson Welles. Poor Marilyn had been such a close friend of his. How they'd all laughed when Peter Lawford had played that trick on Bette Davis! It was convenient how everybody he talked about was dead, or almost. I'd mention that I'd just bought a quilt—my passion—at an auction in Ohio, and he'd launch into this story about Jayne Mansfield throwing a dinner party and how her dress had been ruined when somebody had spilled a glass of wine on it and how she'd gone upstairs and come back down wearing nothing but a blanket.

I didn't know much about those golden days, so I hardly knew if the stories he told could even be true. I did know that Bill would go out to lunch sometimes and come back with a couple of old fashioneds in him, and then he really was impossible to shut up.

I sold some of my own material at the store—quilts and linens mostly—and Bill took a cut. It was those kinds of sales that made it worthwhile for me to work there. One day a woman came in, and I recognized her. She was the moderately famous daughter of a very famous father, and she was very interested in quilts. I was showing her some of my best pieces when Bill came back from lunch.

He was obviously in his cups, and when he managed to find his way to his desk in the back, I heard him start telling Ron, the other employee in the store, more of his stories. Ron knew who our customer was, and he was quietly trying to get Bill to lay off.

But Bill wasn't having anything of it. He launched into a long harangue, one that we'd heard about a hundred times before, and my stomach curled into a knot. I knew that the punch line included a tasteless statement made by none other than our customer's father.

She had been trying to ignore Bill at first, but he was throwing around so many names it was impossible not to notice. I tried to distract her by pulling out another quilt, raving about its detail and the rarity of its pattern and the quality of the stitching. It didn't really work, especially when her father started cropping up in the story. She wasn't looking at me anymore, just staring at Bill, who by now was practically shouting.

"And so Joan says, 'You're nothing but a washed-up, two-bit son of a bitch,' and [he names our customer's father] looks her straight in the eye and says, 'That's better than being a two-dollar whore with a ten-cent rinse job.' "

And the famous daughter just turns and walks right out of the store.

—Colleen, 41, Ohio

● ● ● ● ● ● ● ● ● I BROUGHT MY LUNCH EVery day. I'd put it in a little paper bag and leave it in the refrigerator in the back room. It was a little copy shop, and I worked the counter while Bill, who owned the place, would run the big jobs in the back, the manuscripts and stuff like that.

And about two days a week it was gone. I'd say, "Where's my lunch?" Bill would just look blank. Once he tried to blame it on a delivery guy. But there were just two of us.

Once I even brought some old moldy meat loaf, as a test, but that disappeared too. I don't know how he ate it, because my dog wouldn't touch it.

I wrapped everything in foil, since I thought then I could hear him unwrapping things. But the machines made too much noise. I looked for the empty bags in the trash, but I never could find out what he did with them.

Finally I gave up and started eating out. He must have lost about ten pounds after that.

—Jesse, 44, Wisconsin

● ● ● ● ● ● ● ● ● Y WIFE'S A DOCTOR, TOO, and she's two years older than me. We were lucky and did our residencies at the same hospital, I in cardiology and she in surgery. We don't hide the fact that we're married, but since she kept her last name it isn't obvious from the start.

A lot of my second-year rotations were with the same attending physicians Ellen had worked with. She'd warned me about Dr. Hayes, saying he was a bigoted old fart, and once she was no longer a resident they kept an uneasy distance, since cardiologists and surgeons do a lot of work together. A lot of other people had warned me, too, and it was easy to see what they were talking about.

When we were with patients, he was almost cruel to them, making jokes about their condition, especially to men about their future sexual prowess. And when we were in staff-only sections of the hospital, he let the slurs flow. It had been a long time since I'd heard anybody use some of those words except on TV.

I guess he never figured out that I was married to Ellen. We were in the elevator one day, four or five of us about to start our rounds with Dr. Hayes, when another doctor who could have been his clone got on. I don't remember his name, but right away they're telling dirty jokes and exhibiting other high standards of professional conduct. I tuned out.

Then Hayes said, "What that Guinness woman needs is a good screw." Only he didn't say "woman," and he didn't say "screw." I won't use the words he did to talk about my wife.

I didn't say anything. I really couldn't think of what to say, except something like, "That's my wife you're talking about," which sounded kind of corny. The other residents were looking at me as if they expected me to say something. There wasn't any question he was talking about Ellen, because there was only one Dr. Guinness in the whole hospital. I don't know. I was weak. I stayed silent.

The elevator door opened on our floor and we all stepped out. Down the hall to the right I saw Ellen coming in our direction. Hayes gave her a sneer and headed off to the left. I stayed put. I wasn't really sure what I was going to do.

Ellen saw me and smiled, and then I felt *really* guilty. Just as she walked up to me, Hayes turned around and snarled, "Brown, hurry it up."

And so, with him looking right at me, I grabbed my wife and gave her a big, juicy, wet kiss right there in the hall in front of Hayes and the other residents and a couple of patients who looked pretty entertained.

Ellen was actually not very happy about my turning on the old sex drive with everybody watching. But it was worth it to see the look on Hayes's face.

—*Steven, 29, Indiana*

● ● ● ● ● ● ● ● ● I T WAS ONLY A SUMMER job, but what a summer! Guy's was this little roadside diner down on the Eastern shore in Maryland, not far from Rehobeth. Naturally, Guy was the owner. I was a short-order cook. Guy had the short-order temper.

Man, once this customer complained about the coffee, and Guy stuck his head out from the kitchen through the pass-through and started cussing him out and tellin' him to go to McDonald's.

We had some tables outside and some teenagers were out there, peeling out in their cars for the hell of it and scattering gravel all over the lot. Guy ran out there with this big old kitchen knife and told 'em he'd cut their balls off if they didn't stop. They believed him.

His temper was always ready to explode. The strangest thing, though, came at lunch one day. We were pretty busy, and we had a lot of orders for hot dogs. In fact, we were running out. And it came down to there being one more hot dog than we had a bun for.

Guy just completely lost it, man, he just went loco. He picks up this one last hot dog off the grill with his bare fingers—and that grill is really hot—and he takes it in his hand and starts squeezin' it. There's hot dog coming out between his fingers and out of the top and bottom of his fist. And he's yellin' at it, real loud, so everybody in the diner can hear him.

He screams, "You cock-suckin', goddamned, son-of-a-bitchin', mother-fuckin' asswipe of horse guts." Then he throws what's left of the hot dog against the wall and it slides down behind the fryer.

Four people just got up and walked out without paying after he did that, so you can guess what he was like for the rest of the day.

—*Thomas, 19, Delaware*

● ● ● ● ● ● ● ● ● ● I'D BEEN HIRED TWO months before as a sales rep covering Los Angeles. My interviews had been with a district manager who was promoted to the national office a week after I started. When my new regional supervisor called to announce that he'd be coming down from Fresno to spend a day accompanying me on sales calls, I was nervous, partly because I wanted to make a good impression—this was my first real job—but also because the guy was strange.

He told me that he would just crash at my place instead of staying at a hotel. "We can get to know each other real good," he said. But it was also pretty clear he'd be pocketing the per diem the company gave us all for travel away from home. And he seemed disappointed that I didn't know any great singles bars. Hey, I was new in town and I was trying to get a grip on my job. I barely knew the woman in the apartment next door.

Tom, as I'll call him, showed up at my place on Thursday evening, with a heck of a lot of luggage for somebody just in town for one night. Surprise. He planned to stay through the weekend. Never mind if I cared.

He was a slob. He looked at the photos on my dresser and wanted to know all about my girlfriend in Seattle. He dragged me to the nearest bar, got outrageously drunk, stuck me with the tab, and when we got home passed out on top of my bed. I slept on the sofa bed that I'd put clean sheets on for him.

It was a major effort not to be late for our ten o'clock call. He was grouchy, interrupted my pitches, and kept apologizing to the buyer because I was so new. "Kid hasn't learned the ropes yet," he said. "I'm here to make sure everything goes real smooth."

The buyer was ready to send us out the door with a pitchfork by the time we were done. Tom insisted on eating at a diner that looked like it raised bacteria for penicillin manufacturers. The greasy food hit my stomach like a torpedo. When he was through with the lunch that I paid for, Tom announced that he was still hung over. He wanted my car keys so he could go back to the apartment and sleep it off.

When I gave in after a weak protest, he demanded ten bucks so he could buy some Pepto-Bismol, dropped me at my two o'clock appointment, and told me to call him when I was done.

That call went well, but when I wrapped up about a quarter to five, I was just as queasy as when I finished lunch. I called my apartment, but I didn't get an answer; the machine just kept picking up. I kept calling for about an hour, wasting time in a mall, trying to ignore the fact that I was uncomfortably warm, until I finally decided to walk.

Like I said, I was new to L.A., and I seriously underestimated the time it would take. I got back to my apartment around seven, dragging my heavy sample case and feeling like I'd been ground into paste. I knew I was sick and I just wanted to curl up and get some sleep. Surprise again. Nobody home, and my car was not in the parking lot.

My house keys and car keys were on one chain. I hadn't

hidden an extra key under the mat, the manager wasn't around, and there was no way to get in a window. I was locked out.

I called my few friends, but they weren't home, so I settled down on the stairs to wait, feeling sick and damn sorry for myself. Eight o'clock came. Nine. I was very feverish now and sure I would hallucinate soon. Ten. Eleven.

At about eleven-thirty I saw my car turn wildly into the parking lot, lurch into a space, and screech to a halt. Tom staggered out, and I watched in amazement as the passenger door opened and a blonde dressed in Lurex got out. Tom wove across the lawn, followed by his bored-looking guest, and lumbered up the stairs.

"Hey, kid," he belched. "You didn't have to wait up. Me and Debbie here just got a little lost on our way back from Sunset."

I vomited on his shoes.

—Jeff, 29, California

● ● ● ● ● ● ● ● ● ● I NEVER KNEW JUST WHAT IT was that made Alex hate me so much. I was working in the training program of a New Orleans bank, rotating from department to department. Alex was in charge of the program, and he really went out of his way to see to it that I got assignments that had nothing to do with my interests—departments like trusts or new accounts when what I really wanted to be doing was international.

Somehow I did manage to swing an assignment in international, and I loved it and they loved me. I rotated out of the department after a few months, but I knew that's where I wanted to go. As my time in the program neared an end, I knew I had to find a department within the bank that would hire me. Otherwise I'd be out the door. I couldn't forget, because Alex was always reminding me about how soon I'd be out on the street.

I put in for a position in international, but there weren't any openings. I still had two months to go, so I had some hope when they told me I'd be the first person they hired if anything opened up. I put in for other departments, too, but I didn't really want them like I wanted international. The weeks passed, and nothing came. I got one offer from a branch in Shreveport to do loans, but I let it go.

By this point, Alex was practically gloating. I wasn't even working in the main office—I was at a branch out in Belle Chasse—but he'd make a point of calling me every couple of days, just to point out that I was going to be fired soon if I didn't get a position. I put in a call to the guy in international who'd made me the promise, but he was out of the country. Naturally.

So the day came, and I was "let go." I didn't have a position, and I told myself I didn't really care. A friend of mine had a pretty good import/export business going, and I got into that. We were successful, and I was making more money than I would have if I'd stayed at the bank.

About a year and a half went by and I wound up at a cocktail party given by another firm that we sometimes did co-ventures with. I'd been there about ten minutes when I met up with the guy from international who'd promised me a position if one ever opened. He asked me what I was doing, how I liked it, that kind of stuff. I told him, and he seemed impressed. "You must like it," he said.

"Sure," I told him. "I think I could have had a blast working for you, but that didn't work out, so here I am." I said I owed my friend big for giving me a job when I was out of work.

He gave me a funny look. "I thought you left the bank to take this job."

"No, I was fired when I couldn't get a position after the training program was over."

"I don't know what you're talking about," he replied. "I had a position open up two days before I left for Mexico City, so I had the paperwork done to give it to you. When I came back, Alex told me you'd turned down the job and quit."

So, there it was. I had been offered a position and Alex kept me from knowing. I could have been doing exactly what I wanted to do. I was bitter, but only for about six months. Then oil prices dropped. The bank failed. And they were all out of work—especially Alex.

—*Roger, 33, New Orleans*

● ● ● ● ● ● ● ● ● ● I WAS DIRECTOR OF ARTISTS and repertoire for a small classical recording label. Mort, Jr., had inherited the company from his father, and he knew nothing about classical music. In the ten years since Mort, Sr., had passed away, most of the important artists had left. Mort, Jr., believed that the best way to make money was not to spend any, and the quality of everything had gone downhill. I took the job because I fancied myself a sort of savior, the man who could turn things around and restore the company's lost prestige.

That meant attracting new, upcoming talent, and my best opportunity was Adrian, one of the top agents in the business. She had just taken on a teenage virtuoso violinist I'd heard play in Warsaw a year before. She and I had done good business at my previous job, but when I went to work for Mort, Adrian told me he didn't have the class it took to sell classical recordings. She would never sign one of her clients on his label.

I was determined to change that. I finally persuaded Adrian to meet me for lunch for a serious conversation about signing up the violinist. I booked a table at an exclusive, very proper restaurant and armed myself with our revamped marketing plans and a couple of impressive new releases I'd brought out. Then I made the mistake of telling Mort what I was up to.

"Fantastic!" he cried. "That kid'll be worth big bucks. But you'd better let me join you. Adrian and I go way back! You'll need my help."

I knew they went far enough back that Mort had once pinched Adrian's fanny during the opening ceremonies for Lincoln Center. I tried to talk him out of it, but he wouldn't give in.

So when we walked into the restaurant together, Adrian took one look at Mort, and I felt my stock plummet. I tried to keep the conversation on the things I was doing to revive the label, but Mort kept wincing whenever I talked about something that cost money. He had three whiskey sours before the food came and told a rude story about a famous conductor's taste in young boys. Adrian was fuming and I wasn't getting anywhere.

When the food came, Mort at last shut up and I began my spiel again. I found my rhythm and thought I was making an impression, but then I noticed Adrian was staring at Mort.

He'd ordered steak, of course, and he'd managed to half slide it off his plate while tearing out chunks about the size of golf balls, which he was chewing with his mouth open. His tie was already spotted in three places.

I watched him fork up an industrial-size load of mashed potatoes and lever it toward his mouth. Never a stylish kind of guy, Mort kept strings attached to the earpieces of his glasses so he wouldn't lose them. They were off his face now, resting comfortably on his ample stomach. As the fork approached Mort's wide-open mouth, a large dollop of potatoes slid off and landed square on his glasses. He never noticed.

I stopped talking. It was no use. Adrian waited a moment, then excused herself to go to the ladies' room. She never came back.

—Richard, 41, New York

8

The Deep End

This time it isn't in your head. It's happening, it's getting weirder and weirder, and there's nothing you can do to stop it. You passed the boundaries of decency ages ago, and now you're traveling at jet speed into the realms of madness. There's only one force that holds sway here, only one person who matters, and it isn't you. It's your boss, the one who makes Napoleon look like Gandhi, and you're trapped. There is no escape—only surrender.

HANS WAS FAMOUS FOR being difficult to work for. The saying in the business was that he ought to just install a revolving door, since his employees came and went so quickly.

I took the job as his assistant because I wanted to learn about conference planning. I lasted a year, which was a record for that position.

The problem was his temper. He was a madman. Something would go wrong and he'd go out of his mind. Someone would cancel a seminar or retreat, and Hans would pull a drawer out of his desk and throw it against the wall. When I got there, he only had three left; when I quit, there weren't any.

I was sitting in my office one day, talking on the telephone, and I could hear him ranting. I couldn't understand what he was screaming about—what difference did it make? I was just hoping that the person I was talking to didn't realize what was happening. I heard a crash, and I knew that he'd broken a window. Again.

The screaming got louder. Now my caller wanted to know what was going on, but I said there was just something happening on the street. There was another crash, then a thud. He must have knocked another picture off the wall.

Then, suddenly, there was an enormous curse, and the whole room seemed to shake. I looked up and about two feet away from me, there was Hans's fist, sticking out of the wall.

—Kevin, 25, New York

● ● ● ● ● ● ● ● ● **H**ERE, DARLING, TAKE A rose one. It's for peace and harmony. It'll make your headache go away real fast."

So I sat at my desk for half an hour with a rock pressed against my forehead because Tricia knew all about the power crystals. Each time I tried to put it down she'd rush over and say, "No, no, dear. It isn't time yet." A couple of clients came in and saw me, but they didn't seem to notice. After all, if they could deal with Tricia, how strange was a secretary holding a stone the size of a baseball over her left eye?

Tricia was New Age through and through, and she was nuts. It wasn't just crystals. All the plants in the office had these little pyramids made out of popsicle sticks stuck on top of them because Tricia said that made them grow better. Every day before we started I had to sit down cross-legged with her on this crazy-looking rug. She'd hold my hands in hers and chant some meditation about finding inner peace and creativity. My desk faced the room on a diagonal, and it was about ten feet from the phone because Tricia said that was *feng shui*, the ancient Chinese art of room-arranging.

The digits in our phone number added up to twenty-two because Tricia said it was "advanced." She wouldn't even call me Elizabeth; she said "Liz" was better numerologically for business. I hate being called "Liz."

But the clients lapped it up. One lady had Tricia do her whole house with a pentagram theme because it would bring her power. And for a guy up in Malibu Tricia found somebody to make a set of silverware with tourmalines embedded in the handles because he wanted to awaken his sleeping creativity. Tricia confided in me that this was actually dangerous, because tourmalines are so powerful they might awaken deep anxieties. But if the client wanted it, Tricia was happy to oblige.

I couldn't drink any coffee at the office because it was a "pollutant." And whenever Tricia took me to lunch, it was at this place where they served seaweed pasta in an oat-bran sauce. Yum yum.

But pyramids were really Tricia's big thing. She told me she even slept with one on her head because she found it so revitalizing. We did lots of houses with pyramids in them. One of Tricia's clients had seen a place she'd done in Westwood, and he decided he had to have a giant pyramid suspended from his cathedral ceiling. He also wanted it in a hurry because he was having a party on Friday night and wanted to impress his channeler, who was coming. Tricia told him sure, but at double the price for a rush. He didn't even blink.

Tricia knew this shop where they would make pyramids out of aluminum and fill in the sides with glass. She ordered one about fifteen feet square, and they said they could have it ready on Thursday, which they did. Friday morning they were supposed to take it to this guy's house, and a carpenter Tricia used would hang it.

We went over Friday morning to supervise. Tricia always had to supervise, because normal people just didn't understand the intricacies of these mystical things. I'm sure they didn't. The owner of the house was there, and he was all excited when they unloaded it from the truck, at least until it wouldn't fit through the door, and the carpenter had to take it apart, and it was hauled in through a big window in pieces.

The guys from the shop put it back together, then announced they were leaving, which was a problem. It was clear that the thing was extra heavy, and there was no way the carpenter could lift it himself. Tricia had a big fight with them, but since she couldn't figure out that what they wanted was a big tip, they left.

Well, the carpenter went ahead and installed a heavy-duty hook in the ceiling while Tricia got on the phone to get help. She finally lassoed her son and he drove over, and that was it for extra help.

By this point the client was really upset, and Tricia had to lead him through some meditation until her son arrived. He didn't seem flaky like his mom, and he just sighed and asked her what he should do.

We tried a couple of things, but what it came down to was this: the carpenter on one side, standing on his ladder; the client opposite him on another ladder; Tricia's son on another side, using a chair, a table and another chair as a ladder; and me on the fourth side.

Now, I'm no bodybuilder, so it was pretty clear to me that I wasn't going to be able to support my side, and I said so. But the carpenter told me I'd just have to add stability, not actually lift, because the guys would do that. They pushed the furniture around so I could go from the floor to the couch and then make a giant step onto the top of a small bookcase.

Up we started and, man, that thing was heavy. I made it onto the couch, and then the arm of the couch, and I stayed there for a bit while the guys inched up. I was struggling to climb sideways onto the bookcase without knocking the guys off their perches, so Tricia came over and gave me a boost. I made it, but Tricia scratched my leg with her two-inch nails, and I could feel the blood dripping down my nylons.

Once we had the pyramid up, we had to maneuver it so that the ring in the top would catch the hook in the ceiling. I had to lean pretty far to the left, and suddenly I felt the bookcase start to topple. I yelled to Tricia and she ran over and grabbed my legs. But instead of stabilizing me she pulled me toward her and I lost my grip and fell.

I landed on the couch. The pyramid landed on the floor. The glass broke with a big crash. I lay there for a minute wondering if I was seriously hurt and then I heard Tricia say, "Oh, Liz! You've broken it!"

—*Elizabeth, 28, California*

• • • • • • • • **L**ESTER HAD WORKED FOR Voice of America in Haiti before he came to our station. Nobody knew why he was brought in as station manager, but because the station owner used to work in the Pentagon, there were all these rumors that he was

CIA. He used to disappear for weeks at a time and wouldn't say where he'd been, so that fueled the fire.

Plus, he was real conservative about the news. We were a classical station, and news wasn't a big part of our programming, but Lester spent about half his time making sure we weren't running stories that were "disrespectful" to the President. After a touring Russian violinist came to the station for an on-air interview, her American publicist complained later that Lester had tried to talk the violinist into defecting.

And there was this military tone to the way he ran things. Everything had to be dated military style: "3/5/82" wasn't March 5, it was 3 May. He even tried to get us announcers to say "2200 hours" instead of "ten p.m.," but too many listeners complained and he gave it up. When we went off the air at one in the morning, we started playing "The Star-Spangled Banner."

I guess all this is supposed to explain how strange he was to us and how he didn't understand what a classical station was all about. But he really drove the message home to me one afternoon. My show was usually contemporary stuff: Copland, Britten, once in a while some Philip Glass. That day, I decided to play Blitzstein's *The Airborne*.

I'd just finished a brief summary of Blitzstein's life and goals, mentioning his strong anticapitalist sentiments and his association with the work of that wily old communist Bertolt Brecht. The symphony had been playing about thirty seconds when the door to the booth burst open and Lester barged in.

"Turn it off!" he yelled. "I don't want you playing that music."

"But it's already started!" I protested.

"I don't care. You're not playing it on this station!"

I refused, but he just reached around me and dragged the needle off the record. I cringed as I heard the scratch through my earphones. As I grabbed the mike and started saying something about technical difficulties, Lester grabbed the record. He took his keys out of his pocket and made big scratches over both sides, then threw it on the floor.

Then he turned and walked out.

I cut to a commercial.

—Raphael, 45, Florida

● ● ● ● ● ● ● ● ● ● **E**VIL, EVIL, EVIL, EVIL. There's just no other way to describe her. I was a publicist in New York for a small film studio, and Dolly was the publicity director. She was a bitch in the usual ways—rude, cruel, tyrannical—but what was really disgusting was that she kept a dossier on everybody in the office in this special locked drawer in her desk.

I found out about it because this friend of mine tried to push Dolly to do some extra publicity for this film he was involved in. And when she wouldn't, and Scott threatened to go to the VP for marketing, she whipped out this five-year-old file. An employee had proof that Scott used cocaine.

It wasn't really enough to get him fired, but it would have been an embarrassment, especially since we'd entered the age of the New Sobriety, and people were even putting their dogs in twelve-step programs.

So Scott had backed down and Dolly got her way. But Scott started nosing around, and pretty soon he turned up a whole bunch of people Dolly had blackmailed over the years. She knew who was screwin' who, who'd had an abortion, everything.

Late one night a bunch of us were at the Top of the Sixes having drinks, and we got a little sauced. And, all of a sudden, it was "workers of the world, unite!" We ran out of there and all the way back to our building and up to Dolly's office.

I don't know how come nobody heard us, but eventually we broke into her desk and found these files. They were amazing. She was like Deep Throat. You could tell that over the years she'd cultivated assistants, mail room clerks, people who quit, anybody who had an ax to grind. She even kept track of things like long-distance personal calls from the office.

It was obvious that she was going through people's desks—taking things, photocopying them, and putting them back. In my file was a copy of a card I'd gotten from my boyfriend with a bouquet of flowers, and inside he'd written something kind of sexy. It wasn't pornographic, it was just intimate. I'd never shown it to anybody and I'd taken it home two days later, so she had to have copied it very fast. Even more outrageous, I'd gotten those flowers the day I started.

So now we had the dossiers, but what did we do next? We talked about turning them over to her boss, but then we'd have to admit how we got them. Besides, we weren't sure it was such a good thing if management got their hands on that stuff either.

But we knew we had to destroy them, because they represented too much temptation. So far we'd only looked at our own files. Well, okay, at a few other people's, but only ones we really hated, and we didn't find out anything new. Anyway, we decided to go to this guy's apartment in the Village, because he had a fireplace.

Before we left, we cut up a magazine and pasted together a note that said something like:

YOU've BEEN a very BAd GIRL

IF YOU ever DO thIS again

WE WiLL MakE yoU very SoRRy

Then we went down to the Village and burned every last page.

Dolly never took official action about her desk being broken into. It would have been really easy to figure out from the security guard's log that we all came and left together that night, but I guess she was too freaked.

The end came quickly for her after that. People from every other department got the word that her files were gone, and she quit within a month. Somebody told me recently that she's developed agoraphobia, which means she's afraid to go outside. After the way she terrorized people, she deserves it.

—Fran, 30, New York

● ● ● ● ● ● ● ● ● ● **I**'D BEEN WORKING IN A new job about six weeks when strange things started happening. I had all these hang ups on my answering machine, and then I started getting news clippings in the mail about people who got revenge—lovers who'd been jilted, a woman whose cat was run over by a Dominos pizza delivery man, those farmers in Iowa who shot their bankers. The envelopes were typed, and the postmarks were from all over the region. I was kind of freaked.

At first I thought it was this woman I'd been dating and dumped. She had to be after revenge! But then I thought about it and realized I was kidding myself. Angela was pretty much a straight-arrow, and I was sure I hadn't meant that much to her. I felt guilty for being a sexist pig, but I forgot about it pretty quick when the weirdness got weirder.

I came home one day and my electricity was off. I called the electric company, and they told me I'd requested a shut-off. I straightened that out, but the next day my phone was off. Same story. After I got my phone back, I called the garbage company and told them that I wasn't moving anywhere and that they should ignore anybody who told them otherwise.

The next day I had a call from Jill, the woman I'd talked to at the garbage company, who told me someone had called and tried to get my collection stopped. She was kind of caught up in this, too, since I'd told her my whole story. She tried to get some information out of the caller, but the only thing she could tell me was that it was a woman.

A woman? I knew it really couldn't be Angela. It just didn't make sense, not that any of this did. But Jill convinced me that it really was time to call the police.

They took me pretty seriously, I'm glad to say. I guess there are enough crazies in the world that they have to be careful. They didn't promise me a bodyguard or anything, but they filled me in about having the phone company watch my line, and they told me to save all the clippings that were still coming, since using the mail to make threats was a federal offense.

It wasn't the cops, though, who caught my secret despiser. My buddy Phil lives across the street, and about a week later, when I pulled into the driveway, he came running over with a camera.

"There was this woman sneaking around your house when I came home, man. I remembered all that weird stuff that's been going down, so I booked inside and got my camera. Got her right here," he said, tapping his trusty Nikon. "Got her license number, too."

While Phil drove off to get the film developed at one of those one-hour places, I inspected my house. It looked like someone had tried to pry open the sliding-glass patio door. I went inside, called the cops and gave them the license number Phil had written down.

Phil was back in a lot less than an hour because he'd told the guy at the photo place that it was police business, which I guess it sort of was. Anyway, he whips out the picture, and I look at it, and I know who it is, but I just can't believe it.

I'd quit my last job the day before I was supposed to go on vacation. I planned it that way 'cause I hated the place, and I had an offer to work at a lab that was a half-hour closer to my house. Everybody had been pretty p.o.'d, but nobody was madder than Sandy, the chief technician.

Suddenly, it all fit together. She was one of those still-waters-run-deep types. Sandy talked to herself all the time when she was working, and a lot of it had sounded pretty angry. And then I remembered all those *National Enquirer*s she read on break, and the clippings made sense too.

I let the police take care of it. They told me they paid her a little call with an eight-by-ten blowup of Phil's shot of her walking down my driveway. They told me she was so scared they thought she'd need a sedative. I didn't press charges because it seemed so sad, now that I knew who it was.

So maybe I wasn't so wrong about the effect I have on women. But if that's what I can do to the mousy, quiet types, I'll stick to the wild and crazy kind.

—*Tim, 29, California*

I'M MORE THAN A LITTLE compulsive about a lot of things, but especially my phone calls. I take meticulous notes as I'm talking. Every call begins a new page in a notebook, and I write out the name of the person, their phone number, the date, when the call started, and when it ended. I developed this habit as the only logical response to Harry, my boss.

Harry is a complete idiot. He forgets what he tells you. He changes his mind about what he wants you to do and how to do it. Since we work for a major airline, when Harry screws up, the results are disastrous.

I had a particularly long conversation with Harry one day when he called in from Denver. He gave me detailed instructions about changes in the fare structure that he said had been approved. I wrote a memo based on this conversation and my very-accurate notes and circulated it that afternoon.

The sky fell in. The whole thing was all wrong, and the president was furious. The next morning he came storming over and demanded that I explain myself. I just showed him my notes. He was a little suspicious that I would happen to have such detailed back-up in the middle of a crisis, but when I showed him seven old notebooks full of notes, he believed me.

So Harry took the heat. It was not my fault. I did exactly what he told me to do, and I had no reason other than his natural ability to screw things up to believe that something might be wrong. Nevertheless, Harry decided he hated me. He started criticizing all my work, giving me a hard time about my lunch hour and time off, and ridiculing me in front of other employees.

This was very stressful, so one afternoon I called the personnel manager and told her that I felt I was being persecuted and that Harry wanted revenge. I told her I was afraid that Harry was setting me up to take a fall on something. I told her I thought he was incompetent and that I was tired of covering for him.

She told me she was glad I had alerted her, and that she

would keep an eye out on my behalf. I took notes on all of this.

The next morning there was another screwup, and only because I had my notes was I able to prove that I'd done exactly what Harry had told me to do. He was really angry, and I was glad I'd had that conversation with personnel.

I went to lunch with a friend, but just as we got to the restaurant, she remembered a call she had to make, so we just picked up some sandwiches and went back to the office. I turned the corner into our short little hallway and saw that my office door was closed. I never close my office door. Ever. I walked right up and threw the door open, and I caught Harry red-handed, tearing pages out of my notebooks.

I started yelling and he started yelling, and pretty soon security came, and then personnel. And we both got trotted down to the office of the VP for human resources, where we got a real tongue-lashing.

So what's the punch line? There isn't any, except that I still have to work for Harry, and that he still screws up all the time, and I still have to take notes on everything I do for him. But isn't that what hell's all about, suffering for eternity?

—*Allison, 38, Arizona*

● ● ● ● ● ● ● ● ● ● **I** WAS SUPPOSED TO BE A bookkeeper for a small chain of natural food stores. Steve and Janet owned three of them, and I was hired to do a better job of recording expenses and paying the bills than they had. It was pretty hard, since they didn't seem to think much of things like receipts, promptness or terms. But the worst part was that they'd mistaken me for a gofer. I found myself running to the cleaners, taking their dog, Luke, to the vet, doing their Christmas shopping, and spying on the competition to make sure we weren't charging too much for quinoa, whatever that was.

I tried putting my foot down, but that only had an effect for about two days at a time. If I didn't have a two-year-old to support, I would have walked, but I'd been six weeks without work before I stumbled into this holistic bedlam, and I couldn't afford to get out.

When they announced in February they were taking off for New Orleans for a week, I was in heaven. Now I could get some things in order before Janet sent me out to buy cash-register tape or Steve decided to open the bank statement and absent-mindedly dropped it in the trash.

Two days before they left, though, Janet asked me to go by their house while they were gone, bring in the mail, and feed the dog. I tried to say no, but this time she had the grace to offer me an extra hundred bucks if I'd do it. So I said yes and took the keys.

I'd been to the house before to pick up Luke, and he hated me because I was the one who took him to the vet. They left on Friday morning, and it was Saturday afternoon before I got over there with my daughter, Amy. I expected the dog to start barking as soon as I pulled up; he was a big, stupid mutt and pretty territorial about Steve and Janet's place, even though they didn't seem to give a darn about him. So when I didn't hear anything, even when I put the key in the door, I thought I was lucky. Maybe he was taking a nap.

But no dog. I checked all the rooms, upstairs and down. I even called his name out the back door in case they'd left him in the yard. Then I found him in the garage. He was dead. Luke was sprawled out on a thin blanket on the cold cement floor. He was cold, too, and stiff—clearly dead a long time.

I panicked. I cried. I even tried to give him mouth-to-mouth resuscitation. He had starved to death because I hadn't fed him. He had frozen to death because I hadn't come and let him into the nice warm house. It was all my fault. Of course Amy was bawling, mostly because I was so upset, and I finally just left so we both could calm down.

I didn't know what to do at first, but when I got home I knew I had to call the county and have them take the body away. Bad enough that I had killed Steve and Janet's dog. Imagine how they'd feel if I let the corpse rot in their garage for a week. So

I called the pound and pleaded with them. At last they agreed, probably just to get this hysterical woman off the phone, and I had to go back and watch them toss Luke's lifeless body into a truck.

I spent a week in terror. Steve and Janet hadn't left a number in New Orleans, and they didn't call in. I scheduled three job interviews and considered calling a lawyer in case they sued me, and when Sunday rolled around, I sat in my car in their driveway, waiting for them to pull in.

They seemed pretty surprised to see me. They must have known the news was bad because I burst into tears as soon as they got out of the car.

"I'm so sorry," I sobbed. "It's my fault. I should have been here sooner, but—" They were looking at me then looking at the house for some sign of catastrophe. Finally I blurted out, "Luke's dead!"

There was a pause. Then—

"Honey, we know that. He died Friday morning," Janet said. "I guess we should have called you. But since you didn't have to feed him this week, we'll still pay you fifty dollars for bringing in the mail."

—*Christie, 31, Tennessee*

● ● ● ● ● ● ● ● ● ● **I** HAVE TO ADMIT THAT I felt pretty important when Grover hired me to be a "facilitator." He'd come to town because the symphony was having a big fund-raising drive, and they'd hired him to spearhead it. I don't know who recommended him, but I was in heaven.

The main thrust of the campaign was a benefit concert at which the symphony would perform along with some pretty spectacular talent for a town of a hundred thousand people. Carol Channing was coming, and Tyne Daly and Tony Bennett.

Months before the concert date we sold out the hall with really expensive tickets. I was on top of the world.

Then the cracks began to show. I'd booked hotel rooms for all these famous entertainers, but I'd never had any contact with them or their managers. The symphony's conductor started to pester us about the numbers that were going to be performed and how much opportunity they'd have to rehearse with the stars. Grover got all testy.

Then my mom went to Vegas for a long weekend, and she came back with this flier that said Tony Bennett was going to be performing there the night of our concert. I showed this to Grover, and he said, "Don't worry about it, kid. All the stars take a night or two off during a run."

Which is probably true, but I bet you they don't fly all the way to Alaska to sing five songs with a local symphony for free. So I went to some of the people on the symphony board and told them that I suspected a con. They were *real* upset, but one lady's husband was a friend of the sheriff, and she said she'd have him do a rundown on Grover.

I don't know why nobody did this in the first place, because what came back was a mess. Grover hadn't ever been convicted of fraud, but he'd been arrested for it seven times in Arizona alone. He'd also been out of a mental hospital in Oregon for only about six months before he showed up to "help us out."

At the same time, I made a few calls myself to the William Morris Agency, and to Camden Arts, and to the Agency for the Performing Arts, all in Los Angeles. Guess what? Carol Channing and Tyne Daly and Tony Bennett had never even heard of Grover.

So they arrested him. Most people got their money back, and the symphony board told me I didn't have to give back any of the salary Grover paid me, which was pretty upstanding of them. But I still feel guilty about it, and I'll probably be buying season tickets to the symphony until they bury me.

—*Jerry, 32, Alaska*

• • • • • • • • WHEN VIOLET WAS JUST A buyer for the bookstore she was tolerable, but then she was promoted to manager of the textbook department, and she was like a woman possessed. Which is an ironic phrase, because Violet was a real Bible-thumper.

She was always talking about her church and always trying to get me to come. I already went to church every Sunday, and I liked that laid-back Methodist approach a lot more than Violet's kind of religion. Hers always had her sticking her nose in other people's business, and practically every week she had a new pamphlet that she'd force on all of us.

Violet felt it was her duty to point out the errors in the ways of her subordinates, and she was just as busy in the spiritual world as she was checking the stock in the organic chemistry section. Her first victim was Lee, a college student who worked nights. Lee was gay, and Violet gave him such a hard time that he quit about two weeks after she was promoted.

Then she started on Tracy, who was living with a man who wasn't her husband; in fact, he was still married to another woman. Violet made Tracy miserable by forcing her to reshelve the entire Japanese language section three times in a week. It's hard to arrange books by author when you can't read the alphabet they're printed in, and every time Violet found a book out of order, she'd make Tracy start all over.

Slowly, other people began quitting, and real fast it was clear that Violet was replacing them all with people from her church. Most of them were perfectly nice, and good workers, but pretty soon all the conversation was about bible study and the evils of the liberal local school board. I was the only member of the old staff left within six months.

Violet kept after me to come to her church or maybe a sing-along they were having, or to bring my kids to their vacation bible school. I refused politely each time, but I began to grind my teeth. Why couldn't she let up? Besides, I missed Lee and

Tracy and everybody else. They'd been good people and I liked them.

I thought maybe summer term would be easier since the bookstore hours were shorter, and for a while it was. But I hadn't counted on the 1992 Republican Convention. After that ugly first night when Pat Buchanan declared a cultural war, I went into work with my head full of angry thoughts about small-minded people.

It was like I'd walked into a revival meeting. Everybody else was positively gleeful. Old Pat had really shown America the way, and George Bush was going to lead us out of moral decay. Violet was completely energized. All morning long I kept hearing, "Praise the Lord!"

At lunch break Violet and I took over the cash registers. Summer term was over, but fall was starting in a week and a half and a few students were already coming in and buying textbooks. As I finished ringing up one young man, a young woman went to Violet's register with an armload of books.

I recognized most of them as texts used in the women's studies classes. Violet had a very dim view of women's studies. She started ringing the books up, moving through the stack like she was touching poison. Then I saw her pick up a collection of lesbian erotica with a rather suggestive cover.

"This is disgusting!" she spat. "How can you bear to read such filth?"

The student looked pretty taken aback. This was, after all, an assigned text for a course. "It looks all right to me," she said.

"It's degenerate. I won't sell it to you," Violet announced.

Now your average college student has pretty firm ideas about things like freedom of speech and the press, and this young woman just looked Violet in the eye and said, "You have to!"

Violet stuck the book inside her cardigan and folded her arms across her chest. "I will not! It is an abomination against the Lord!"

"I want to see the manager," the student announced.

"I am the manager," Violet retorted.

"I'm calling my professor!"

"Go ahead."

Well, I'd had just about enough myself, so I said, "Miss, go get another copy of the book and I'll ring it up for you."

"Benjamin! You will do nothing of the sort!" Violet shouted.

"Go on, I'll sell you your books," I told the student, and she scurried off.

I reached over to pick up the other books from Violet's counter, but she threw herself on top of them with her arms spread.

"Benjamin, you will not sell these books to that girl or anyone else!" she growled.

"Violet," I told her, "this is a university bookstore, and our job is to see that the books are stocked and to sell them, not to decide what people should read."

From her position on top of the pile of books, Violet growled, "If you sell her those books, you're fired."

I laughed. "Violet, if you try to fire me for not selling an assigned textbook because it offends you, you're going to be the one who gets fired. The board will laugh in your face."

Violet just started singing some hymn I'd never heard, and I sold the young woman all the books she needed. Pretty soon a crowd had gathered to listen to Violet sing, including some of Violet's fellow churchgoers, who looked extremely embarrassed. The stationery department manager came back from lunch and saw what was happening, and he went and got the general manager.

But Violet wouldn't let go of her books, and finally they had to get two campus security officers to escort her home.

I'm the manager now, and some of Violet's friends still work here. So do Lee and Tracy again, and we're all very happy, thank you very much.

—*Ben, 38, Pennsylvania*

● ● ● ● ● ● ● ● ● **B**ENNY WENT AWAY ON vacation for a week, to what he told us was a relaxation seminar. He needed it. He shouted, he slammed doors, he hung up on clients. Winter, King and Herring was a very tense law firm before Benny Winter headed up to the Sierras.

When he came back, he seemed a changed man. The little lines around his eyes were gone, he didn't turn red anymore, and when Marge asked for an afternoon off so she could check out some day-care centers for her son, he said, "Sure, do whatever you have to do to be responsible for your life."

We thought it was just kind of creepy at first. Benny used to be the kind of lawyer who'd bully someone into accepting a deal, but now I heard him saying things like, "Hey, I hear where you're coming from, my friend. I see your space."

Then he announced that he was taking all four members of the secretarial staff out to lunch. We were in total shock. Benny made us pay for the coffee in the office pot! We went to this nice little restaurant, and he was all friendly and asking us questions about our lives.

Linda mentioned that she and her husband were probably getting a divorce. He didn't want her to work anymore, and they were fighting all the time about his kids from a previous marriage. That's when Benny let the cat out of the bag. This place he'd gone to hadn't been just a spa, it was run by these people who'd once been part of est but had "seen a better path."

"You'll never know real peace until you've been there," he said. "You'll see that we're all troubled by things we don't understand at first. We want power, but we're all in the grips of someone else's power. We have to throw off the chains of unrealistic expectation and learn to discover our own true wants and fears."

He went on like this for about twenty minutes. All kinds of mumbo jumbo about finding our baby self and learning to suckle it. It was kind of gross. Then he took these books out of his briefcase and gave us each one and told us to read it by next week. We were all going to have lunch again and talk about what we'd learned.

I read about ten pages and quit. I don't think anybody else got much further. It was all about guilt and anger and power, and I thought, if anybody needed this stuff, it was Benny, not us.

At lunch the next week we all just stared at our plates when Benny asked us what we'd discovered. He kept asking these embarrassing questions about how we felt about our parents and how we felt about him. Nobody said anything except "yeah" or "maybe" once in a while.

He was pretty disappointed. He told us maybe we were afraid of what we'd discover about ourselves if we really thought about this stuff. I thought that was pretty rude, but I didn't say anything.

Alice King, one of the partners, asked me what these lunches were all about the next day, and I told her. She looked pretty upset. I don't know how she hadn't noticed how strange Benny had been acting, but she told me she'd take care of it.

They had an awful fight. It started out quiet, but after they'd been in there an hour, I could hear Benny yelling again, just like the old Mr. Winter we'd all known and feared. They were still in his office with the door closed when we all went home.

The next morning Benny called me into his office. He looked all peaceful again, and he started in with this stuff again about how I had so much to learn and how I shouldn't resist what he was trying to teach me. I told him that I felt just fine about my life, and I was happy with the spiritual guidance I got from Rev. Claiborne every Sunday. If he felt better, that was good, but this stuff wasn't for me and I didn't want to go on any more lunches.

That's when the old Benny Winter came back. "Listen," he hissed at me, "this isn't just some lamebrained preacher stuff. This is powerful. It was thought up by really deep thinkers who know a hell of a lot more about life than you ever will. It's the best kind of thinking there is, and you'd better get used to it or just maybe there won't be a place for you here any more."

I walked straight out of there and into Alice King's office and told her I didn't have to be insulted like that. Then there was an even bigger fight, and Mr. Herring was yelling at Benny, too.

Alice told us all to take the day off, and when we came back the next morning, Benny wasn't there. Now it's King, Herring and Greenspan on the door, and the last I heard, Benny was in Minnesota at one of those places where you dry out.

—Karen, 25, California

● ● ● ● ● ● ● ● WORKING AT A 911 DIS-patch center is really tough, because all through your shift you've got people calling with emergencies. You're the only help they've got, and they expect you to do something right away. Sometimes you've got Priority One calls stacked up, and no units to send out, and then some old lady will call to complain about this guy down the block who's playing his radio too loud. When you tell her that someone will be there eventually, she starts screaming about her taxes and how she wants a police car *right now*!

The other people on my shift are really terrific, caring people, and they take what they do seriously. One woman had this guy on the phone and his apartment was on fire and he was trapped. She dispatched the fire department right away, but she stayed on the line with him because he was absolutely terrorized—talking to him and telling him to stay down out of the smoke and to breathe through a wet cloth. But he was a goner, and in the end she could hear him screaming until the line went dead. When they found him, he was crisped.

So it's a pretty high-stress job. And they give you counseling and support, and for the most part the county really backs you up. But there was one supervisor, Steve, who was a real bastard. He used to be in law enforcement, and like a lot of those people, his whole life was wrapped up in this tight little world of 911. All his friends were ex-cops, and all he ever talked about was cop stuff.

Sometimes when people get out of these really strict jobs where you're supposed to be ultralegal and really clean, they overcompensate for being free. Steve started dealing drugs, and most of the time when he wasn't on shift he was either drunk or high.

I guess this made him feel really guilty, because he started playing policeman with the rest of us. He would come by our houses without any notice and sit in our living rooms and give us lectures about staying away from drugs and people who were losers. And all we could think of was, well, here's a perfect example. For a couple of weeks he was even following one guy around in his car, like he was doing surveillance.

We reported him to the dispatch station managers, and they came down on him pretty hard, and for a while it stopped. But then one day I was having this party at my house, and a lot of my friends were there, and so were my parents.

Bingo! The front door flies open like it's been kicked, and Steve jumps into my living room. And he's got a gun, and he's waving it around, and he yells, "Everybody down on the floor, you're under arrest!"

Man, we dropped. I was only about ten feet away from him, and I could see from his eyes that he was seriously coked. He also kept sniffing, another clue. My friend Mark, who also works dispatch, tries to start talking to him, using the techniques we'd been taught for dealing with seriously crazy people on the phone, but Steve yells "Shut up!" and fires a shot into my ceiling.

Then he starts into this speech about how we're all dog scum, and he knows it and he's going to haul us all in for all kinds of stuff, like drugs and giving alcohol to minors (I think two of my eighteen-year-old cousins had been drinking beer).

And we just lay there frozen. What else could we do?

But my mom, she was in the kitchen when it happened, and she called 911 as soon as she heard that shot. Man, I have never been so proud of those dispatch people in all my life. It only took about two minutes before we heard sirens.

Steve just started laughing when he heard them, telling us that this was his backup. When the cops got there, they pretended to be going along with him until one of them got his gun, then they hustled him out of there pronto.

I never saw him again after that, because there wasn't even a trial. His public defender got him committed for long-term counseling and observation. I don't know when they'll let him loose, but let me tell you, it'll be too soon.

—Barbara, 37, Ohio

● ● ● ● ● ● ● ● **H**ER NAME WAS MERCEDES, and she was twisted. I mean this woman had deep psychological and physiological problems, and she took them out on anybody nearby, which most of the time was me.

She was the buyer for junior coats and swimwear, and I was the assistant buyer responsible just for coats. Judy did swimwear. Merchandise would come in, and we'd unpack and put it out on the floor on these big heavy fixtures. And Mercedes would stand there and watch us set up the whole thing, and then she'd say, "I want those over there." We'd complain that the fixture was too heavy for a couple of women to move, and she'd scream "Move it!" So we'd move it, though we'd practically get hernias. She didn't seem to care that we wanted to have kids someday. I think she wanted to neuter us.

She would accuse us of stealing merchandise before it ever got to the floor, even though she watched us unpack it. She would have screaming fights with her husband on the phone in the middle of the sales floor.

But the worst of it was when she *really* lost control. Usually, this would happen when we'd go down to Seventh Avenue to the fashion market, and the manufacturers would parade their lines around, and Mercedes would try to cut deals. She was always trying to get them to agree to take back anything that didn't sell. Fat chance.

Anyway, one day we've called on this company that makes swimsuits, and this is when teeny-weeny bikinis are in, and the fashion is to mix and match the tops and bottoms. The company has all kinds of stuff to sell that fits the bill. At first, Mercedes thinks it's a great deal, and they settle on the major points. Then, as they're talking over the details, you can see the change come over her.

One minute she's thinking, this is a great deal. Then it's, this is a good deal. Next comes, this is an okay deal. Then she decides that it's not so hot, and finally she realizes it's a stinker.

And the way you can tell how this is happening is the tic in her left eye. It starts out kind of faint, and it almost looks like maybe she got an eyelash stuck in it and she's trying to wink it out. But then it speeds up, and it's happening with more force. And more of her face gets involved, so that her left cheek shakes every time her eye twitches.

But the eye is really just a countdown to blast-off. Because once it's really going, she starts to yell about how they're trying to screw her and they don't know who they're dealing with.

Now once Mercedes starts to yell, she develops the shoulder action. This time it's on her right side, and it starts to jerk up and down in a completely different rhythm compared to the eye. The more it goes on, the more it gets some front and back as well. Pretty soon, she's standing there yelling at this guy while she's twitching and jerking to beat the band.

And this poor guy she's been negotiating with, he doesn't know what to do. He can't look her in the eyes because one of them is hopping around like a jumping bean. And her shoulder is practically percolating.

This wasn't the first time we'd seen this. At first, Judy and I had thought she was having a seizure, but when we tried to get her to lie down in a dressing room, she tried to hit us. We kept wondering whether she needed medical attention. But Mercedes was so overheated, she didn't even seem to notice that she was having a fit.

So meanwhile back at Fashion Avenue, Mercedes is still attacking this poor man, and Judy and I are just sitting there watching. What were we supposed to do, say "Excuse us, don't mind her, she's mentally ill"? Finally Mercedes stomps out in a big huff and we follow, absolutely mortified.

I know it wasn't just Judy and me who couldn't take this kind of stuff, because when I quit a month later, I had my exit interview with the divisional manager, and the first question he asked me was, "Are you leaving because Mercedes is crazy?"

No. I was leaving because I was afraid she was contagious.

—Christine, 37, New York

9

The Extra Mile

*For service above and beyond the call of duty your
only reward is—more service and make it snappy.
Your spouse has left you, the dog thinks you're a
burglar, and your mother just walked past you in
the grocery store. You've been working so long and
so hard that if your name weren't on the mailbox
you wouldn't recognize your house. Are there
other jobs out there? Who has time to read the
paper to find out? Have you lost your perspective?
Of course not, you're just giving the boss his due.
Don't forget who writes that check!*

● ● ● ● ● ● ● ● THIS WAS IN 1939. I WAS A lieutenant in the Salvation Army, working in San Diego. Our captain was Frank O'Malley, a man who took a distinct dislike for me despite the work we were called to do together. I think this was perhaps because I was engaged to be married to a man, also a captain, who was working in San Pedro. We were to be married in a few months, and I would leave San Diego to join my new husband in San Pedro.

I was actually a Canadian citizen, although I had applied for American citizenship. This would not have normally caused a problem, except that our work sometimes took us over the border into Tijuana, Mexico. It was easy for Americans to come and go into Mexico then, but because of the war in Europe, as subjects of the British Commonwealth Canadians did not enjoy such freedom. Passports and visas were necessary, and crossing was difficult.

Captain O'Malley insisted that I make frequent trips into Mexico and that I lie about my citizenship. I spoke like an American, so no one would question me, he said. I was very unhappy about this dishonesty and the needless risk at which I was put, but Captain O'Malley made me go.

On one trip, just a week before I was to marry, he accompanied me, and as we returned across the border, our bus was stopped by the Mexican police. An officer boarded the bus and asked all American citizens to raise their hands. Captain O'Malley nudged me with his elbow, and since I had already entered the country under a falsehood, I raised my hand.

The officer left the bus for a moment, and then he was replaced by a man who was obviously more important. He demanded to see identification from everyone on the bus.

Of course I had nothing from an American government office except entry permits for a foreign citizen; everything I possessed was from Canada. He moved down the aisle, checking everyone, and when he got to me the sham was exposed.

I was arrested there on the bus and led to a jail, where I waited for two days with rats and insects until my fiancé and other Salvation Army officers were able to secure my release. Unfortunately, I had to be deported back to Canada, where a cloud of suspicion postponed my reentry into the United States. My wedding was of course delayed, and when I did finally return to California, I married my fiancé at once. I never saw Captain O'Malley or heard from him again, and for that I thank the Lord.

—Edith, 87, Arizona

• • • • • • • • **J**AMAICA! I GOT TO SPEND A week there, and Jack paid for it. All I had to do was check out a couple of charter boats he owned, make sure everything was kosher, visit his bank, exchange some documents, and then I could play.

I went swimming, I lay on the beach, I met this really sweet guy who also lived in Charleston, and it was great.

I'd hit the bank on the first day, taken care of the business there, and handed over a file case. The guy Jack did business with gave me some papers back and a box full of computer disks. I didn't pay any attention to the stuff; I was a real estate agent in Jack's firm, and all this was just sideline business to get a free trip.

The boats were fun, doing great business, and I had a blast. I left on Tuesday afternoon and flew back into Miami. I'd bought a few gifts for my family but they weren't very expensive, so I figured customs would be a breeze.

But all of a sudden one of the dogs started barking and three customs agents whipped out their guns and pointed them at me. They dumped all my stuff on the table and started tearing it apart. They ripped open the lining of my suitcase, they smashed all my cosmetic bottles, and then one of them opened the box of computer disks. Out tumbled a pile of dark green stuff, and I was busted for smuggling marijuana.

—Eleanore, 38, South Carolina

● ● ● ● ● ● ● ● ● I 'M SLEEPING COMFORTA-bly after twenty hours of labor. I've delivered a happy, healthy daughter, and I've drifted off very contented in the thought of spending the next six weeks with her, let alone the next eighteen years.

Then there's a hand shaking my shoulder. It's the nurse, I think, just checking in. "I'm fine," I murmur, and try to snuggle a little deeper.

"Marge, Marge, wake up."

I open my eyes, but it's dark in the room. I know it's daylight, but the curtains are drawn.

"Whaddizit?" I mumble.

"Marge, where did you put the file on the Tollner merger?"

—Marge, 36, Pennsylvania

• • • • • • • • E DNA WAS THE BUYER FOR European couture of a major Fifth Avenue department store and I was her assistant. I was about as interested in five-thousand-dollar gowns as I was in getting hit by a truck, but if I survived a year with her I could get into the company training program and move to menswear.

It amazed me that Edna managed to hold onto her job. She couldn't remember anything, she couldn't tell an Armani from a Dior with a magnifying glass, and she dressed off the rack from Alexander's. Size sixteen. I managed to keep track of the things she told me about, but every week there were missed appointments, shipments that arrived which no one was expecting, and loud screams from accounting about lost bills and contracts.

Somebody upstairs eventually decided to pay closer attention and told Edna they wanted to look over the incoming fall lines. But Edna didn't tell me, and one fateful day I arrived to find her in a panic. "Get me some models!" she screamed. "We've got to show these gowns at eleven!"

Where? I wondered. I managed to get four good-looking assistants from other departments to volunteer, but there was no way they could model all those clothes.

"Andy, you've got to help me!" Edna wailed.

What else could I do?

Edna called cosmetics, she called the personal buyers. She even tried the Ford Agency. They laughed. It was ten-thirty, the whole store knew what was happening, and we were clearly sunk.

At ten to eleven I found Edna wedged into a Valentino with a frilly skirt that stopped about halfway to her knees. She looked like Hulk Hogan in a maid's uniform. "We're all going to have to pull together on this one," she announced. Then she pulled a full-length sequined number off the rack, held it up to my chest and said, "Here. You wear this one."

We were both fired at eleven-oh-three.

—*Andy, 23, New York*

● ● ● ● ● ● ● ● ● ● **I** WAS SUPPOSED TO BE IN charge of leasing out the hall for outside events, anything put on by groups that were not a part of the permanent consortium of organizations that used it most nights. That included charity benefits, recitals sponsored by local universities, that kind of thing. My predecessor had been very unorganized, and I was the opposite. Everything flowed smoothly. To Carol, who was the president of the foundation that ran the hall, that meant I should take over anything else that was a problem.

At first she tried to stick me into things like publicity or negotiations with the stage crew. But there were already people doing those things, and they screamed bloody murder. That was fine with me. Just because I did my job well didn't mean I didn't have anything to do.

But every time something out of the ordinary came up, Carol made me deal with it. It was a real drain.

Then she decided we would have a management retreat. All the upper echelon would go to this resort down on the Delaware shore and talk about ways we could work together better. I think she read something about it in *New York* magazine. If they did it in New York, we could do it in Philadelphia.

So guess who got put in charge of the arrangements. Carol kept changing the list of people who were going, so I had to keep shuffling room reservations. Of course, nobody wanted to share, and this person couldn't stand to sleep in the same room with that person. It was a real mess.

And of course at the last minute she decides it's getting to be too expensive, and she cuts the list even more. That really made the hotel mad, and everybody thought I was the one who'd cut them off the list, though it was beyond me why anybody wanted to spend a weekend with Carol in the first place. Then she told me I wasn't going either, but I just sighed in relief.

So it's Friday, and people start getting to the hotel about noon. And it's a disaster. The rooms aren't ready; the conference room is too small; they don't serve any vegetarian meals. My phone rings off the hook all afternoon, both our people and the hotel people.

Finally I flee home about six o'clock, fix myself a stiff drink and sit down to watch a movie. I fall asleep in front of the TV, and when I wake up it's because the phone is ringing. I can see by the clock on my VCR that it's after one o'clock. I kind of panic because nobody would be calling at that hour with anything but bad news. I think maybe somebody's dead.

Worse, it's Carol. She's very upset. There weren't seat belts in the back seat of the car that drove her down. She could have been killed! The hotel won't let them have their meetings in a sunny corner of the restaurant, where she's sure people will be much happier. Someone sent her a fax and it wasn't delivered for two hours. What if it had been an emergency?

What she wants me to do is call the hotel conference manager—right now. I point out that it is rather late and the poor man has probably gone home. That's okay, because she has his name and she already got his home number from information. She's going to sit right there by the phone until I straighten all this out and call her back.

What else could I do?

—*Carlotta, 36, Pennsylvania*

● ● ● ● ● ● ● ● ●ET THIS REPORT FIN-
ished on time, Carol, and it'll mean a big promotion for you."

I replayed Ted's words constantly in my head for three weeks as I prepared the analysis of the performance of our three new clothing stores. The chain's growth had stalled for two years until we'd opened new branches around Miami. They were working like gangbusters, and it was my job to tell the company why. I slept about three hours a night; blew off my new boyfriend—the smart, handsome one who loved my taste in music; ignored my friends, and grew big, ugly, dark circles under my eyes.

Ted would call me every day to check up, really putting the pressure on, tantalizing me with stories of a new office, my own secretary, a company car. The stress made me a madwoman. My goldfish died of neglect. Even my mother quit speaking to me. But I finished the report, and I knew it was a great job.

Monday morning I walked into his office and handed Ted the report. The grin on my face was a mile wide. I was already planning a vacation in Europe and mentally admiring the view out my new window. I didn't really notice the cardboard box on the floor with some picture frames and a coffee mug in it. Ted looked at the report's cover sheet for a second, then handed the whole thing back. "Thanks," he told me. "But I just quit this job. Show it to the next guy."

—*Carol, 29, Georgia*

• • • • • • • • W E CALLED HER "BABY" BE-
cause that's what her daddy
called her. Daddy was publishing a business directory for some
of Chicago's better suburbs, and Baby was supposed to be in
charge of selling ads. What she was really good at, though, was
getting her hair cut.

Baby would drop into the office about eleven, leave for lunch
about noon, come back at three with lots of shopping bags and
go home at four. She sold three ads in six months, all to friends

of hers who owned cute little stores that sold cute little things to Baby's other friends.

Baby had a rough life. Her BMW was always in the shop and she had to drive a Toyota, which was really unfair until Daddy got her a Lexus, too. She was dating this guy named Rod, and he was really cheap and he wouldn't take her out more than twice a week unless she whined. Luckily, Baby was good at that.

Mostly she left the advertising staff alone, but I was her assistant, and the truly unfair thing was that if I sold an ad, Baby got half the commission—as if she needed it. Daddy paid the bills on her gold AmEx card anyway.

Poor Baby, she had to work so hard on upkeep, and those women where she got her facials were so rough. Then her hairdresser quit and moved to Florida, and nobody could get her hair the same color he could.

One day Baby was in her office and I heard her curse. "Jeremy," she called, "come in here."

So I went in, and Baby was sitting there with her right hand held out in front of her, her fingers spread apart. There was a bottle of nail polish on the desk.

"I'm so clumsy," she said. "I keep getting this stuff all over my left hand. I was supposed to have my nails done today, but I just don't have time. I'm meeting Rod for lunch and they look so awful."

She stuck out her left hand and by golly there was a little spot of actual nail showing on her index finger. I nodded my head and kind of smiled.

She picked up the bottle of nail polish in her left hand and held it out to me. "Here," she said, "you do the left one."

And I didn't get a tip, either.

—*Jeremy, 25, Illinois*

● ● ● ● ● ● ● ● T WO YEARS I SLAVED FOR that man. I was an idiot and he was a coward. We'd built a book club for music lovers from the ground up. I wrote brochures and assembled a panel of respected musicologists to review our selections. I typed invoices, I kept records. I ordered office supplies, I made sure the copy machines worked. I don't know what he did, but I worked evenings, weekends, holidays, all because I thought we had something that was going somewhere.

After the first year things seemed to be going all right. The membership was growing; we got computers and hired a secretary and a few part-time people to handle orders. I was reading books like mad, I lunched everybody in the business, and then Dick told me he wants his daughter, Lisa, to start writing the brochures. She was in publishing. She understands these things, he said. Like I didn't.

And then he started timing my lunches, complaining if I took more than an hour. Who has a business lunch in just an hour? He complained about personal phone calls—like my friends could call me at home. I was never there; I was always at the office. And, of course, all the time it's "Lisa says we should do this." "I talked it over with Lisa and she disagrees with you."

But the worst moment came when it was time for raises. I made my recommendations about the staff's salaries and he accepted them. And then I said, "You know, Dick, we haven't talked about my salary."

"You?" he said. "You're not getting a raise."

"What?"

"I don't think you're really interested in this job anymore. You argue with me all the time and you don't work as hard as you used to."

"And when were you going to tell me all this? Next year?"

"I thought you realized you didn't deserve a raise."

Then I really blew my stack. "You coward. You want me to quit, don't you? You wanted me to do all the dirty work, to get this business going so then you could bring in your little princess. Why couldn't you have handled this like a man? Why couldn't you tell me you were unhappy with me? Why couldn't you just fire me and give me a severance package? Admit it, that's what you want!"

He just sat there, cowering, sweat rolling off his forehead. He wouldn't answer me. He couldn't answer me.

So I walked out to the secretary, borrowed her typewriter, and typed my letter of resignation. Then I went back into his office, slammed it down on his desk, and walked out. For good.

A year later he sold the company to somebody who could make it work. I still get membership solicitations from them. And they're still using the brochures I wrote.

—Sue, 37, New York

● ● ● ● ● ● ● ● **G**ARY RAN HIS OWN IMPORT/ export business. He'd bring stuff in from all over the Orient, mostly cheap junk made by virtual slaves in steamy little sweatshops. A lot of the people he did business with had offices in Seattle, and he spent a lot of time being chummy with them.

One night he went out with a bunch of businessmen from Korea, and they went from bar to bar, drinking it up. They finally ended up at some sleazy strip joint, and they drank way too much, and when the bill came, nobody had enough money to pay for it. At least, that's what they said.

So Gary left his American Express card and told them somebody would be in the next morning to pay the bill and pick up the card. I got to be that somebody. I was the gal Friday as well as the bookkeeper, the mail room and the receptionist. The only problem was, Gary had had so much to drink, he couldn't remember exactly where this place was or what it was called.

So I spent half the morning calling his drinking buddies trying to find out where they'd all gotten so snockered. And because Gary was so cheap, I was supposed to find out if any of them had sent somebody down to pay the bill. Of course they hadn't. But about ten-thirty, one of them at least remembered the name of the place.

Off I went, except that Gary decides I should just tell them to bill the company of his drinking buddies and he'll sort it out later. Right. And of course at eleven in the morning this place isn't even open yet, and I have to stand in front of a strip joint for forty-five minutes before somebody lets me in.

And will they give me Gary's AmEx? No. Will they bill his buddy's company? No. Will I pay a $185.00 bar tab out of my own pocket? No.

So it's back to the office, where Gary has a fit. "Don't you realize that I'm leaving for Hong Kong tomorrow? I have to have that AmEx!"

Back I go with a check. But the manager wants cold hard cash. For some reason he doesn't trust Gary.

And of course Gary starts swearing at me over the phone when I call him. And the customers in this place are giving me the creeps. They're all seedy, bleary-eyed businessmen. They keep staring, and they probably wonder why I keep coming back and pleading with this scumbag manager. Eventually I get a check from Gary, cash it at the bank, go back to the strip joint, pay the bill, get the AmEx, and walk to the door.

Which opens. And in walks my ex-boyfriend.

—*Pam, 31, Washington*

● ● ● ● ● ● ● ● ● ● **I**T'S THREE O'CLOCK IN THE morning and my phone rings, all right? I lunge out of bed and grab it, and it's my boss, Marvin, who's in London.

"Hi, Stacey, I hope I didn't wake you."

Sure, like I was just sitting here doing my nails.

"What's wrong?" I mumble.

"I forgot the file on the Edgemere project. I have a really big favor to ask. Could you fax it to me?"

"I guess. I'll do it as soon as I get in."

"Well, actually, I need it pretty soon. I have a meeting with Peterson in three hours. Could you go down to the office now?"

I groan. "Marvin, it's three a.m. here."

"I know, I'm sorry, but it's really important. If I don't have that file the whole meeting will be a waste."

So I give in. I put on some sweats and go out to my car, only it won't start. Usually I call my father when this happens because he only lives five blocks away, but I don't think he'll appreciate a phone call right now. So I take the spare keys to my dad's car and I jog over to his house. Along the way, it starts to rain really hard, and by the time I get to Dad's house I'm soaked.

The car's in the driveway and I get in real quietly, but not quietly enough, because the dog starts to bark. I can't drive off now because I know that as soon as that dog starts to bark my father wakes up. So I ring the doorbell, only my father doesn't answer.

I think maybe this time he's sleeping through it, so I go back and get in the car and start it up. Kerpow! There's a shot, and I see my father in the doorway with his shotgun pointed right at the car.

It takes me about ten minutes to calm him down, standing there in the rain, and he's still pretty upset when I finally drive off.

It's almost half an hour to drive to the office, and when I get there the security guard won't let me up because I've forgotten my ID. I've never seen him before, and he's never seen me either since I don't usually come in at four in the morning. And I don't blame him for being suspicious of some woman who shows up soaking wet in sweats looking like hell.

I tell him to call Marvin in London—he'll give permission for me to go up—but the guard won't do that because he's not making a transatlantic call. He's probably never made one in his life.

Finally I bully him into letting me up and I run to my office.

The file isn't there, and it isn't in Marvin's office. I know I packed it for him, so he must have left it at home. I wonder what else he left, but I'm too busy taking things out of other files, putting together everything that I can remember is related to Edgemere.

By now it's almost five-thirty. I call Marvin's hotel in London to get their fax number, and I tell them to let Marvin know that I'm gonna send the fax through. But it won't go, because their fax line is busy. I call the hotel back, but they only have one fax line. Marvin's not in his room either. I figure he's down at the desk, driving them crazy about this fax, so I keep trying and trying for an hour, and it finally goes through.

All this time I'm calling Marvin's room, but there's no answer, and I can picture him having a fit and firing me when I finally reach him. About seven o'clock, I decide to go home and change.

It's rush hour now, and instead of half an hour, it takes me an hour to get back to my dad's and drop off the car. I drag him over to my house, and there's a nasty note behind the screen door from my friend Jill, who I was supposed to car pool with at eight o'clock. My dad starts to fuss with the car, and I go inside to get changed in a hurry. Then I head back to the office, and it takes me another hour to get there.

It's nine-thirty now, which means it's two-thirty in London. I call Marvin again, but still no answer. I finally get to have a cup of coffee after being up for six hours, but I can't get any work done because I'm all spaced out, and I feel like I'm getting a cold.

After lunch there's a message that Marvin called, but I still can't reach him for the rest of the day. I go home early, about four o'clock, and go straight to bed.

About eleven-thirty I wake up and wander into the living room to see what Leno's doing, and that's when I see there's a message on my answering machine. I don't know when I looked at it last because I've been running around. I hit the play button.

"Stacey? Stacey are you there? It's Marvin. I only talked to you about five minutes ago. You must be in the bathroom. Listen, I just found the Edgemere file in my suitcase. I don't know why I put it there. Anyway, don't worry about faxing me that stuff, 'cause I've got it right here. Talk to you soon, babe."

—*Stacey, 31, Maryland*

● ● ● ● ● ● ● ● **M**Y GIRLFRIEND BECKY AND I went to St. Tropez for a romantic weekend. I booked us a really nice room in a big hotel. I could imagine long walks on the beach, some good sailing, a romantic dinner, and then I'd pop the question and she'd say yes.

It was a disaster before we even got there. In Miami we were standing in line for our connecting flight and I heard a voice behind me. "Mark, buddy, how's it hanging?"

I turned around and standing right there in white shorts and a shirt open down to his navel was Chuck. Chuck wasn't my immediate boss, he was my boss's boss, and he worked in the main office in North Carolina. I hardly saw him except maybe three times a year. But we were fated to be best buddies on the trip.

He slapped me on the back and started talking. "Heading off for the islands, huh? Great time of year, lots of chicks coming down. Fantastic action. You ready to score?"

I introduced Becky and he didn't even blink. "Pleased to meet ya. You got a great guy there, Beck. A real comer. He's got a great future in the furniture business."

I hated the furniture business. I'd told Becky I wanted to quit but she thought I should stay in. She gave me a satisfied smile.

For the next twenty minutes we listened to Chuck talk about himself. Then when we got on the plane he just sat down next to us and kept talking. The guy who actually had that seat wanted to sit there because it was an aisle seat. Chuck's seat was next to a window. There was almost a fight and the flight attendant came. Chuck finally paid the guy a hundred bucks to change seats with him.

"I hate sitting next to people I don't know. You can never get a decent conversation going."

Not that we had a conversation during the long, long flight. We listened to an oratory. Becky tried to go to sleep on my shoulder, but it was no use.

When the plane landed, I thought we could ditch Chuck, but oh no. He was staying at our hotel. At the reception desk he tried to get a room next to us, but the clerk could see the look in our eyes and she put Chuck at the other end of the hotel on another floor.

We ran for the elevators, and we thought we'd escaped. But as soon as we got to our room, the phone rang. Guess who?

"Step out on the balcony," Chuck told me. I did it, and there he was, three floors down, about ten rooms away, waving at me. "See, we can still find each other real easy."

Great. I told Chuck that we were going to take a nap. Becky lay down, but I went down to the gym and worked out. When I came back Becky said that Chuck had called three times to find out when we wanted to have dinner.

We had room service, which wasn't exactly romantic, but Becky's got a good spirit, and pretty soon we were in bed and it was nice and we were forgetting all about Chuck.

Bang, bang, bang. We didn't answer, but he kept knocking. "Hey, you guys, open up," Chuck yelled. We just hid, and he only stood there for about ten minutes. Finally he said, "Well, you must really be going at it. I'll find you later."

End of the good mood. Becky said she had a headache and I believed her because I had one, too. We watched *Backdraft* on TV and went to bed.

We got up early the next morning and had breakfast by the pool. We decided to take a boat out because that seemed to be a good way to escape Chuck, just us and the deep blue sea.

But he must have had radar, because as soon as I'd signed my name to the bill at the dock, Chuck came running up. "Hey, you wouldn't go anywhere without your buddy Chuck."

I was tempted to spill all of us into the ocean and pray for sharks, but Becky didn't swim that well, so we only spent about an hour out, listening to Chuck's riveting stories about furniture sales before we headed back.

"I'm starved, let's get something to eat," he insisted, so we were trapped by the pool with him. He whistled at the women and drank two piña coladas. No food.

Becky saved us for a while because she wanted to rent mopeds, and Chuck wouldn't ride them. We rode all over the island, and our good mood started coming back. We did a little shopping and had a quiet lunch, just the two of us.

Back at our room, however, the little red light on the phone was blinking, and Chuck had called five times. Why didn't we meet him for dinner at five?

Instead we got a reservation at a restaurant in town. We took a cab in and sat down to some primo seafood. I had the ring in my pocket, everything was going great, and as I thought about what a champ Becky had been with Chuck I knew all over again that she would make me so happy if she said yes.

Dessert came, and I was fidgeting with the ring in my pocket. I started to tell Becky how glad I was we'd come, how I really liked spending time with her—especially without Chuck. She even laughed when I said that. Good old Becky. I'd even said the big *l* word for the *second* time that night when we heard it.

"There you are! Man, I've been looking for you guys all over this island. Didn't you get my message? Boy, am I starved."

Chuck pulled up a chair, ordered a steak, and we couldn't dump him for the rest of the night. We got to bed at two, after they threw us out of the restaurant before Chuck could have Mai Tai *numero cinco.*

I got up early the next morning and ran down to the lobby. I pounded on the florist's door until somebody let me in and sold me a bunch of flowers for a small fortune. I hurried back upstairs and set the flowers on the table next to Becky with the ring inside the little envelope. The note said, "Marry me, and I'll take you away from all this." Then I climbed back into bed.

I heard Becky wake up and gasp when she saw the flowers. I heard her open the envelope and I felt her sit down on the bed. I rolled over and she looked at me and she was crying.

"Oh, Mark, I knew you were going to do this. I . . . I . . . I mean—"

Bang, bang, bang.

"Hey, you guys, rise and shine."

I saw the light go out of Becky's eyes. She stood up, walked over to the door in her underwear, and she opened it. There was Chuck. He looked like he was getting a real eyeful. Before he could even close his mouth Becky yelled, "Chuck, get lost!"

And she slammed the door in his face. Then she walked back to me, gave me a long, sweet kiss, then pulled away.

"Yes, on one condition."

"Anything."

"Quit your job!"

In an instant, sweetheart, in an instant.

—*Mark, 28, Georgia*